Stephen

Intuitive
Lovers

Lots of

Love

Becky

First published by O Books, 2010
O Books is an imprint of John Hunt Publishing Ltd., The Bothy, Deershot Lodge, Park Lane, Ropley,
Hants, SO24 0BE, UK
office1@o-books.net
www.o-books.net

Distribution in:

UK and Europe
Orca Book Services
orders@orcabookservices.co.uk
Tel: 01202 665432 Fax: 01202 666219
Int. code (44)

USA and Canada
NBN
custserv@nbnbooks.com
Tel: 1 800 462 6420 Fax: 1 800 338 4550

Australia and New Zealand
Brumby Books
sales@brumbybooks.com.au
Tel: 61 3 9761 5535 Fax: 61 3 9761 7095

Far East (offices in Singapore, Thailand,
Hong Kong, Taiwan)
Pansing Distribution Pte Ltd
kemal@pansing.com
Tel: 65 6319 9939 Fax: 65 6462 5761

South Africa
Stephan Phillips (pty) Ltd
Email: orders@stephanphillips.com
Tel: 27 21 4489839 Telefax: 27 21 4479879

Text copyright Becky Walsh 2009

Design: Stuart Davies

ISBN: 978 1 84694 316 4

Printed by Digital Book Print

O Books operates a distinctive and ethical publishing philosophy in
all areas of its business, from its global network of authors to
production and worldwide distribution.

Intuitive Lovers

Becky Walsh

BOOKS

Winchester, UK
Washington, USA

CONTENTS

Foreword

This book has been born out of a post-coital comment, "you are too much in your clitoris". My defensive comic wit spun back with "well at least one of us is", but the wound to my ego was deep. I was a "sexpert", knowing everything needed to pleasure my partner and myself; I could play any role, spent many hours hearing about technique from Gay male friends. I was technically brilliant and emotionally retarded.

In my defense, I was a victim of my age, reading too many women's magazines on how to find the perfect handbag and lover in the same aisle of the supermarket, telling me the route to happiness was to become independent in every way. The female evolution into masculinity was in full swing. What did he mean too much into my clitoris!? But the truth was that my full attention was focused on orgasm. My consciousness had shrunk to the smallest tip of my darkest place. My consciousness needed to expand, not just into the rest of my body or my partner but also into love itself. Needless to say my defensive ego ended this short relationship and started the long journey to non-ego-based, intuitive, open love (which, by the way, leads to great sex).

My career is an interesting one to describe. I am a psychic, but I don't predict the future; I use intuition as a tool to have a deeper understanding of the clients that I counsel. By being able to look into the relevant aspects of my clients past, I see where blocks have originated from in the same way a psychotherapist would from talking to the client. I then use a form of spiritual guidance, motivation, inspiration and life coaching to move the thinking from blocks and fear to becoming loving and open. Most of my consultations are about relationships; understandably so, as a relationship is one of the most profound and at times enjoyable/painful routes to spiritual growth. Through another human sharing our life we learn who we are. In fact we

1

become who we are.

Through many years in consultations with wonderful clients I have become increasingly aware of how ready for change we all are, to move from an ego-based, emotional exchange to a conscious open loving connection.

It feels to me that we are fed up with feeling alone and disappointed by love as if it's some force outside of ourselves that we can't control. Most of us are waiting for someone else to give us the love we want, so we feel safe to give our gift of love. For me the only way to feel safe enough to 'be the change' in a relationship that you would like to experience is to be intuitive and open to honestly listening to our partners and ourselves. Love is ever expansive when the ego doesn't put limits on it.

Relationships allow us to grow into the best of ourselves, if we allow them to. This would ultimately change the future of the world. Happy relationships = balanced children.

I dedicate this book to all the people I have shared my lovelife with. But it wouldn't be a misprint if I missed out the f and called it a love lie. I thank you for everything you taught me, and apologize for never having loved you to the best of who I can be.

Acknowledgments

Big thank you to all the people who shared their story with me for this book, you know who you are.

Also to Andrew McMillan, Kate Orr, Anna Kamau, Elouise Carden, Andrea Marcou, Buddha on a Bicycle Covent Garden, Cat Hammond,Caroline Mylon and Cindy Shearer at Ciis San Francisco.

To Louise Weston, the only woman who can still make me blush.

To James Topping, you take your time but you always deliver.

To the brave John Hunt at O Books and all the team there, thank you.

The girls in the bus at the retreat in France, great inspiration.

Front cover photo by Emilie Fjola Sandy. With thanks to Emma Reyes, Joseph Robinson and Coco de Mer. Mask design and crafted by Hoi Chi Ng for Coco de Mer.

Introduction

Your task is not to seek love, but merely to seek and find all the barriers within yourself that you have built against it.
A Course in Miracles

Sex is intuitive. We were born knowing instinctively how to do it. If we had no sex education and no discussions with our friends and family, we would still find out how to make love. Procreating the human race is in our biological make-up.

In fact there is SO much talk about sex, we are bombarded with images and cultural stereotypes. If we hadn't been told all about sex we maybe might be able to enjoy it more! When we are thinking and analyzing our partners and our own performance while making love, we lose touch with our body. Our body allows us to feel our emotions. To be in our analytical mind we lose touch with everything else and making love becomes an act of sex that you do, because it indicates you are having a successful relationship, but the closeness of that relationship, through sex, is lost.

We live in a world where we lack the personal connection in many aspects of relationship building. In our lifetime we have seen the Internet grow into the most amazing way for people to connect to each other. But also in this lifetime when people ask us for directions in the street they don't smile or say thank you. We are faced with news broadcasts of the horrible things humans can do to each other and we hide behind a screen of communication. I love the Internet and with every change that happens in the world we will adapt; my concern is that we may adapt to have a fear-based, passionless life, where we choose our sexual partners by using our heads to work out who is the best person for us and not by using our passion, our heart and our intuition.

Is our evolution bringing us to a place where computer-arranged marriages, built on logic, are the next stage forward? We have a choice; we can decide to choose a partner with our heads or our hearts.

Trusting and understanding your Intuition is the key to becoming fearless in the choice of relationship and people you allow into your life.

Intuition is also the key to:

- Not needing to ask dumb questions, imagine instead of asking 'what are you thinking?' (Which normally means "you've gone quiet, do you wish you were somewhere else other than here with me?"); being able to feel what he/she is thinking.
- To know when your partner was having an affair and not just wonder if was your own paranoia.
- Being able to tune into a person's intention when they have done something to hurt you and feel how intentional or unintentional it was.
- Being able to have the best sexual connection with a person so their orgasm feels like your own.
- Developing the transformation of your sex life to become healing, connecting on the highest level. Leaving behind the sense of the individual into a sense of being whole.
- It can also be a gateway to levels of spiritual enlightenment, bringing together the mind, body and spirit as one.

Our love lives have fallen into pattern with our time. When a person wanted to meet someone in the 1950's and 1960's they would make their relationship connections on average at a much younger age than today. They might meet at a dance; they would smell each other, and be able to feel their energy through touch to know if they had sexual chemistry. The only time we get this close now is on public transport and it's unlikely we will be feeling any sexual chemistry and the smell won't be that great either.

It feels like time is speeding up and the race is on to not get left behind. So we race forward in our careers to get the stability we are seeking. It often feels that our happiness is somewhere out there in the future just waiting for us to chase it down.

In our modern world we judge by putting everything in brackets as either good or bad, right or wrong. These terms have grown now with regard to sexual relationships into 'healthy or unhealthy'. A healthy sex life is one where both partners are satisfied, a woman by at least one orgasm and a man by his stamina. The other measure for 'healthy' is how often a couple has sex. This leads to a focus on the physical act of lovemaking and leaves out the emotional. Women feel pressure to tick the sex box along with the waxing, diet and detox. We live in a very busy world that will judge us by the label on our handbags.

On the road to getting life right, we believe we need the right partner. That right partner will tick all the right boxes at the right time in the right way and if they don't, it means our right life is wrong. Then we need to finish the unhealthy relationship with the unhealthy person and get everything that we rightly deserve, in someone new.

It's a fear of getting it wrong that makes us feel we need to control our lives in order to get it right. We know relationships need work: forgiveness, tolerance, patience and understanding; but few of us have the time to give those gifts to the 'wrong' person. Our mind can become clouded with thoughts governed by fear. The one thing that can give us the clarity is to trust and know our own intuition.

I have decided to present this book in parts. Each part of the book is relevant in some way to each person reading. Even if you are in a long-term relationship you will still find aspects in the first part on meeting a new partner which have useful information. Each section is designed to take you through the many aspects of intuitive love. From meeting a partner we grow into physical love, which is that first flush of attraction and desire, often exciting and full of anxiety. We then grow into emotional love which is an exchange of gifts, one that is easily brought out of balance if it doesn't grow into the last stage: conscious, transformational, ever-expanding love. I have also included sections in the book to allow you to explore some often judged and misunderstood sexual practices and alternative viewpoints. Do what you will with these ideas, they are merely there for you to see how your judgment buttons get pressed and to question if these ideas are your own, governed by collective popular conscious or your own free, educated mind. If we can stop putting things in boxes of right or wrong, then we won't be putting ourselves in the same labeled boxes. Love is transformative; it doesn't sit well in boxes.

Why another book on relationships?

Nearly everything that exists in our lives today came about by human imagination. Imagination has been dismissed as a childhood talent for making up games and storytelling, and yet everything we have ever created came from this root source of our imaginative minds. When people describe something as being 'just' their imagination, they are seriously underestimating one of the most important human tools: the ability to create something that hasn't ever existed before. Many people disregard intuition and put it down to their imagination, as if the imaginative part of the brain isn't worth much and it is therefore safe to disregard intuition. However, both imagination and intuition are the powerhouses behind the secret of humanity. Imagination is the cinema screen for all of our creativity, ideas, concepts and intuition. It is our link to the creative connection we have to God. If God is a loving creative force, then we also have a much smaller aspect of that creative love inside of ourselves. To me, this is how manifestation (also known as cosmic ordering) works. We all have the ability to create our own reality through our imagination.

In our imagination we can dream our life without the experience of past hurts. We then manifest that reality by following our intuition to guide us to the choices and decisions we make with our heart. What blocks our dream becoming our reality is our belief in what we think the world is about. We gain this from our past experiences. Our imagination can lift us from beliefs based on negative expectation into a hopeful future.

This blast of imagination was how the universe first began. It is understood by many that a magnificent, loud sound described as the 'big bang' started the beginning of the universe. To put this in non-scientific terms, imagine if you were just one focus of energy. As this one energy you don't vibrate, you are simply 'being and stillness'. You of course would have no concept of the fact you are 'being and stillness' as we only know what we are by understanding and experiencing what we are not. You then had a crazy idea, what if you could experience yourself? At the exact moment of thought you split and split and split as each atom then has the intention of experiencing itself. Because the energy you are is a creative force everything you think comes into being; to experience what you are you have to understand what you're not. Everything became a polarity of opposite energies circling ever traveling out and back in on itself.

The big bang was this energy splitting in two, the ego-illusion-self and what it always was; this creative being. The ego-self isn't real; it is there to teach us what we are not. What we are not is an individual; we are all part of the 'one' that is experiencing duality to learn what it is not.

Deep inside on some level we know this, and we crave the comfort and the communion with lovers, friends and family because when we hold another's gaze and we see the light in their eyes that reminds us of being one, we know we are at one with each other. This is the unity we feel when we fall in love. The Fear-based-ego would stop existing if we truly understood this feeling of unity and being as one. We get a taste of it in our lovers and the ego panics and brings in all sorts of insecurities, fears, mistrusts and self-development sabotage, to keep us feeling that we are better off staying separate from love and each other. The ego-self would die if we had a conscious understanding that we are all one. After all if we made the realization through our relationships that there was the possibility of being joined with one other person we could be joined with everyone, bringing about peace and the love we wish we could find in the world. The ego fears letting go of what it thinks it is; all the achievements, everything it has worked for, everything it has learned. The ego believes it is the body, the thoughts and the emotions. We are more than our ego, so much more. In a sense we are already in the most complex of relationships. We are in a duality relationship with ourselves, the relationship between the ego and the spirit. Often so intense, no other love could find a way in past the pain bodies the ego creates to defend itself from transpersonal forgiveness and release.

Relationships are one of the keys to the transformation from the ego into the creative-empowered-self. No wonder we are so scared of relationships. The ego brings out our fear and our doubt in others. The unity of making love can really make you feel that sense of oneness beyond the physical body.

At this time we are going through a real shift in consciousness, and intuitive lovemaking seems like as good a way to raise our consciousness as any and it beats sitting on the side of a mountain with your legs crossed.

Rebalancing the masculine and feminine polarity
As part of this consciousness shift we are collectively moving from the predominantly masculine energy into the feminine energy.

The women's movement is a wonderful thing, but we have lost the masculine and feminine energy balance. I believe in having balance and equality but both women and men are now struggling to find their feet in a world of sexual equality, which is also trying to find its feet. We wouldn't want to go back to the 1950's when the masculine and feminine quality was obvious. Men were logical, unfeeling with a strong sense of who they were – 'Men were men' as the saying goes.

1950's women took care of the home and the children; they were in service to their husbands. Women are no longer dependent on men for money or anything else. But they seem to still hold tight to their fear of that dependency, of being vulnerable in some way. Which often means a woman may adopt more masculine energy and attitude. Being open in a relationship is about being vulnerable. The biological role of a man is to protect. We are moving away from our natural biological make-up, and wondering why we don't have the same dynamic of attraction.

'Where have all the strong men gone?'

Many women are desperate to find a strong man, but we always attract our balance. If you are a strong woman you will attract a man weaker than you. Think of the north and the south poles' magnetic energy or a plug with the live spark and the earth wire. One will ground the other in a good way. It doesn't matter which plays which role, but many women wish for a man who will grip their hair and kiss them hard. Can that man also have taste in shoes?

If you want to attract certain qualities in a person or want your partner to change, you have to first let go of those qualities in you. This also goes for same sex relationships. The attraction is the polarity between the masculine and feminine energy. These energies can be found in both men and women. If what turns you on is a macho man then you can't be a macho woman.

Which of the list below do you identify with at home in your private life and in the work place?

Masculine	Feminine
Doing	Being
Effort	Freeness
Active	Passive
Dynamic	Stillness
Thinking	Feeling
Head	Heart/Gut
Intellectuality	Emotionality
Left Brain	Right Brain
Rationality	Sensuality
Positive	Negative
Penetrating	Yielding
Seen	Hidden

Taken from *The Alchemy of Voice* by Stewart Pearce.

From looking at the two lists of words you might see yourself as being more masculine at work and more feminine at home, or the other way around.

When we let go of our dominant side, we are saying that we trust our lover.

We trust our woman to take care of the home and make it beautiful, we trust our man to lead and take the direction.

Sadly what turns you on in the bedroom often turns you off in life. A woman who is a divine feminine may need to talk to her man when he doesn't want to. A strong man who can throw a woman on the bed and make passionate love might be uncommunicative and won't discuss the household jobs.

Even over time a relationship will become a partnership and with it goes the sex life. We will talk in Part Three about how to keep that balance in long-term relationships without losing your partnership bond.

The Ying and Yang energy divide is paramount to all sexual

relationships, and the attraction of them into your life.

The white stag

A short story of the dance between the masculine and feminine takes from the view of a woman's life journey.

The natural tendency for a man is to be a hunter. We see this in the sport they like to play and watch. We see this in the way they view maidens and how they hunt them down on a Friday and Saturday night in packs. Maidens are often Deer-like, big eyes and smooth faces. Open to the world. The hunter hunts the Deer with the bow and arrow. She knows this bow is the same as Cupid's bow: once struck by the arrow, life will never be the same again. Cupid is often depicted as a baby; this is because it is Mother Nature who wants the maiden to become struck by the arrow. This arrow has a poison that makes her mind go gooey; it becomes full of endorphins that make it impossible for her to concentrate on anything but the possible union and connection with the hunter. For Cupid, his job for Mother Nature is procreation of humans. So he warns her by being depicted as a baby. Many maidens run from the arrow and so the natural chase between the hunter and the Deer begins.

Some Deer fall, and although the hunter will delight in devouring them and their rebirth into a stronger woman, he may carry on with the chase. Some Deer are desperate for the dizzy delight of love and will lie down joined by the weaker hunter who will not draw his bow. But if he doesn't pierce her heart she will not stay with him. Some join in a divine union between the masculine hunter and the feminine Deer and stay in a balance of those polarities together.

In time things change for the hunter and the hunted. The Deer becomes wise and at this point she leaves her maiden years and becomes mother. Not all Deer have fawns, or have found their hunter. In the mother years the Deer has another choice, to become extraordinary, or to wish back for her maiden years with crazy face creams to bring back her big eyes and smooth face. She may long for the days when she didn't even know how powerful she was when the hunter chased her and the potential of a pierced heart was always round the next tree stump. At this time from the maiden to mother many Deers stop running and start chasing. "Take me, pierce me, choose me with your arrow, I was wrong to run all this time". It's not always because she wants to be a mother, but she longs for the divine union she has tasted but isn't living the dance between the masculine and feminine energy. However, time often can make the Deer the hunter and she stands proud with the other hunters, who dance with her as men can dance with each other. Others lie down and wonder why time after time the same thing happens, the hunter lies with her, but doesn't pierce her heart. The hunter still wants the feeling of conquest of a magnificent prize; some keep chasing hoping to bag a prize much younger than possible to truly keep. Some are not so interested in the running after fulfillment anymore. The young Deer gave good chase, but untimely didn't satisfy him; when caught, it just wasn't enough.

But wait, there is something in the trees, mystical and mythical; the braches move to reveal a white Stag. Female in energy, the Stag isn't a hunter, but sort after by the male energy of the hunter as a winning prize. She doesn't run, she holds her ground, and with a tempting majestic flick of the head she glides off into the trees. The chase is on. But her majesty has bewitched the hunters; they drop their bows and just run after her. The fittest and the most worthy is in the lead. Weaker men drop away as her power feels hopeless to them. In the clearing the white Stag has stopped. She drinks from the water of pure emotion. The hunter, exhausted from his chase, does the same, and in that moment the hunter merges with the white Stag and becomes Herne the God of the forest. The hunter rides the Stag. She is the goddess, and he knows that she may lock horns with him and she may throw him off her back if he doesn't serve her in the way she demands. But the Goddess knows that they are a match. She opens to him and allows him to ride her feminine divinity as a reward for his service. Herne's service to her is to always keep her warm with his love, to be her protector and her support. His role in her life is to give his greatest gifts to the union and to the world, so she may look upon him as her God. He must let the other Deer run, he may chase as she knows he wouldn't ever choose another over her divinity, but if he ever draws his bow, she will cut off his head. They balance the male and female roles in a unique dance of both coming from the best of themselves. They allow each other majesty to grace the world, as equals they feel no jealously for she has the night and he has the day.

Part One: Physical love

We bond our bodies together and reach for the physical and sometimes emotional release of orgasm. Intuition allows us to experience each other's orgasmic pleasure and know how to touch and be sensitive to the emotional and physical responses of our partner. Ultimately making us better lovers.

Getting a Date

In my work as an intuitive life-guide, I meet people almost everyday who are finding it difficult to meet someone. I truly sympathize as modern life means we are too busy to waste time meeting the wrong people and don't trust strangers. You do have a choice. You can use your intuition to know who you can feel safe and free to meet, or you can sit back and feel helpless and wait for the universe to plan a car crash where you fall in love with the driver of the other car involved. Now is the time to move into your power and bring your relationship future into your own hands.

Here's some face to face ways you can meet people, which will hopefully result in you feeling empowered by your positive action and possibly have a really great time while doing it:

- Host a "White Elephant" party for single people. Everyone who is invited must bring a single friend, preferably of the opposite sex.
- Join a meetup group in your area. Many of these are now listed on line. In the US try www.meetup.com.
- Do a charity event, such as a sponsored walk or a bike ride.
- Find singles magazines or newsletters in your area and join their mailing lists.
- Read the local events in the free newspapers you get through the door and GO to the events that interest you.

- Take a friend or go alone, but just try to meet at least one new person when you go, even if they are the same sex; who knows who you can meet.
- Take a dog to the park even if it's not your own. There are dog owners meeting clubs, which is a great way to meet people who have an interest the same as you. I have a dog and if a new partner doesn't like dogs, we will never work!
- Take an adult education class.
- Your place of work is good if you don't have to work directly with the person that interests you.
- Browse specialist bookstores, libraries, and films shops in the sections that interest you. Ask someone his or her opinion and see if conversation develops.
- Become a volunteer for something you are passionate about.
- Turn up to every event you are invited to.
- Attend art gallery and museum openings and functions.
- Join a health club or sporting team.
- Travel! Consider singles holidays and events. Get away from where you know and go somewhere unknown even in your own country.
- Join spiritual or religious groups.
- Go and see live music and theatre.
- Speed dating is twenty or more people in a room, ten men and women. They have three minutes each to talk to a person and then move on. If you are intuitive, three minutes is more then enough time to feel a connection.
- Don't forget to ask your friends to introduce you to people. They might not think to offer, so ask.
- If you are open to love of life itself, romantic love will find you much quicker.

I doubt that anyone could do this whole list and fail to meet someone they really like. You might not feel like you have the confidence or have inside of you what it takes to do anything on this list. Small steps go a very long way. Ask for help from friends and family. Every journey, to a better life, starts with small steps. I know one lady who bought two tickets to an event she really wanted to go to. She put an ad in the newspaper "free ticket for this concert, my guest must fit the following criteria..." She got men who liked the same concert she liked applying, so they already had things in common to talk about and she found her husband this way. Just a simple step to put an ad in the paper then run with the reaction it creates and be brave. I know you might feel 'it's difficult' and at times exhausting but in truth it's only as difficult as you make it by thinking it's difficult and it wouldn't be exhausting if you met someone you liked. What you think about your life has profound impact on how it plays out. Be the person who chooses what you want to experience, and let go of feeling a victim of circumstance.

Spotting the right face in a crowd or over the Internet

Men and women are different. It's not only the shape of our face or body that makes us different; we really start out life in different ways.

Women's brains are hard-wired to be able to read faces. Baby girls have a need for mutual eye gazing to develop the mother-infant bond. Girls are interested in emotional expression, which lasts into adulthood. A feeling of self-worth comes from seeing in another's eyes that she is getting whatever she is doing right.

Boys don't do this kind of eye gazing as much. Boys experience testosterone surge in utero that slows communication development, so as a baby it's not as important to them to connect with others.

So we have all been face readers of some description our whole lives, but women started from day one out of the womb.

You don't have to feel that you have any amazing intuitive skills to be able to read a face, it's a case of knowing a few tips and making some observations, knowing of course that there will be exceptions to every rule.

Face reading is the idea that the facial features of a person can tell you things about their personality. I remember hearing the urban superstition that you can't trust people whose eyes are too close together. I have found through life experience that people who have close set eyes tend to be narrow-minded and very focused, which doesn't fit my choice of person as a partner.

By using face reading skills you can see if a person is what you are looking for before you go to the effort of reading a profile on the Internet or walking across a bar to talk to them.

The eyes are the windows to the soul. So if you can't see yourself melting into that person's soul don't waste your time! I'm not a fan of colored contact lenses for this reason; it's hard to see the soul past the fake color.

It's a good idea to choose someone whose face is resembles your own. They are likely to find you more attractive. This isn't because they, or you, are in love with themselves but more because they feel connected – almost like people from the same 'tribe' (hopefully not the same family!).

Women also tend to go for people with more of a baby face; the rounder the face and eyes the more we seem to want to take care of this person. Maybe this comes from the need to look after children.

Men's faces

Eyes
Dark eyes mean the person is very deep and thoughtful, which is great, long and interesting conversation. But if conversation is not what you are looking for, try a guy with ice blue eyes; these men often have high sex drives!

Nose
If you meet a man with large nostrils it's likely he will be generous, but won't be able to hold on to money. He is also going

to be fun. Thin nostril types are great with money; they just don't spend it!

Lips

Guys with full lips are very open and honest, great at conversation and great kissers! Thin-lipped men are often great businessmen.

Men with a strong dip between the nose and the lip are very likely to be great lovers. So are guys with short, wide chins.

Women's faces

Ears

Women with large earlobes are likely to be extremely grounded. So when she says she is happy to have no-strings-attached sex, she is likely to mean it, and not call you twenty times asking why you didn't call.

Small earlobes say that the person's interests are more mind-to-mind than body to body.

Eyebrows

Thick eyebrows show a woman who finds it hard to stay faithful. A person with thin eyebrows shows little interest in sex. Curved are very sexual and sensual. Straight eyebrows have more conventional preferences in bed.

Nose

Long, downwards pointing nose has a large appetite for sexual adventure and unusual lovemaking. Bumpy nose can be inhibited and prudish at times.

Mouth

Small-mouthed women are said to be undemanding and passive in bed. They are also quick to climax into orgasm. Large and full lips can be very passionate. Thick upper lips often feel insecure but are an expert at seduction. Thick lower lips often choose unfaithful partners and are then tempted to be unfaithful themselves.

Most women wear make up without knowing the origins of

why we first started painting our faces. Red lipstick is said to give the impression of the blood rush in the lips of the vagina when a women is aroused. At the most fertile point in a woman's monthly cycle she will also have a slightly redder cheeks. Of course if a woman wears a bit of rouge on her cheeks she can fake her fertility and attract a male.

Gay or straight hands?

It is possible to be able to tell if someone is gay by his or her hands. Of course there are exceptions to every rule but lesbians are said to be more likely to be left-handed or ambidextrous and have a ring finger longer than their index finger. Gay men are also most likely to be left-handed. The theory behind this is that when the part of the brain is being formed in the womb for sexual orientation the fingers are being formed at the same time. The two seem to then become linked in their development.

Internet dating

Internet dating is currently the most popular way to meet someone. We now find our relationships in the same way that we buy our weekly shopping. We search for almost everything, including love, online; houses, holidays, books, music, mortgages and cars. The reason is simple. We have become isolated and the old face-to-face methods of meeting people are often harder to find the older we are. People are being single much longer due to careers, and becoming single through relationships breaking down later on in life.

In our isolation from family due to people living all over the world and missing their cultural social groups, the need to have a connection with a special person is even greater. It seems to me that being intuitive about a person is even more important when Internet dating, so you don't waste your time on dates you will have to reject or be rejected by.

The initial assessments we make when we meet someone for

the first time are quite hard; we assess if we would like to go to bed with the person, if we will fall in love and if we want to spend the next 40 years of our life waking up next to that person. We ask ourselves these questions on the first date! No wonder there is so much pressure.

Having the viewpoint that you are looking for the right one for right now will lead you to only one of these questions: "Would I like to spend the rest of the evening in your company?"

You will have probably decided that within a few seconds of meeting the person on an energy level. Deciding if you would like to talk to the person for the rest of the date, and so after sex, will determine whether you go through with having sex (that and how big a glass or two of wine you might have).

Looking for the right one for right now might seem flippant when you are looking for someone to have a family with but no one works well under exam conditions. You want to find a partner to bring children into the world in a joyful loving relationship. So looking for a serious relationship might give you just what you are looking for. Who wants a serious life?!

Falling in love isn't about sexual attraction, or two people with the same viewpoint on life. It's about finding someone who lightens up your day. Think of being that for someone else before you start assessing if they could be that for you.

To get to that first meeting you will have had to have seen their profile online, taken a look at their photo and then started chatting via mail, gotten them off the PC and onto the phone as soon as possible. Then you are not wasting energy in sending mails. It is possible to learn everything you need to know about a person just by looking at their photo. They say that when you star in a photo, part of your soul gets taken; I don't think this then means that people like Kate Moss are somehow lacking parts of their soul but I do believe that the photo holds an aspect of a person's vibrational energy which you can tune into.

How to tune into a photo

Print the photo (as large as you can without losing quality) from the Internet onto photo paper. Doing this will mean that you have a good copy of the image, but also if your reaction is "I can't be bothered", then you have possibly already unknowingly read the photo, or discovered a clue as to why you are currently single!

Hold the photo in your hands, look into the eyes and say in your mind "who are you?" Feel what emotions you have in your body. Do you feel happy and relaxed, or anxious and irritated? If you're not sure put a hand on your heart and ask again "who are you?" Allow your eyes to rest on the person's eyes in the image. Let yourself fall into them as much as possible and make a mental note of any images you get. You might want to go on some exploratory dates with people you didn't get great reactions for, just to see how right you are. You can trust your intuition; how many times do we think when meeting someone "I knew it!"

You are also welcome to test this with friend's photos of people you don't know. It works; it might seem judgmental, but reading people often is about making a judgment about them. It's not a negative judgment about them, more a judgment about what is and isn't for you.

Myers Briggs personality type

We often believe that we are looking for one in a million when we are looking for a partner. Odds like that can seem like a needle in a haystack, but if it's one in a million at least there are a few million in every city. So in a few square miles' radius there could be three possible hopefuls.

We look for a magical, chemical, emotional, spiritual, sexual, logical link to someone, but we can also find that it can be psychological!

The Myers Briggs personality theory developed by Carl Jung, Katharine Briggs, Isabel Myers, David Keirsey and others helps us find people with whom we are statistically more likely to be compatible. This feels like quite an interesting way to look at personality types. It's important to remember when you do this test that no one person is better than anybody else. So if you get called judgmental, try not to take it the wrong way. Everything said is positive. This is seen as a very truthful way to understand your 'core' type. This will hopefully lead to your core match. At least you know others who have gone for this opinion are quite likely to be truthful and intelligent people. Have a look at www.typetango.com for more information.

Manifestation / The law of attraction / Cosmic ordering

Manifestation has become a spiritual buzz over the last few years. The law of attraction simply says that you attract into your life whatever you think about. Your dominant thoughts will find a way to manifest as events in your life. I have a strong belief in the law of attraction and I find the best teachings in it to be from Jerry & Esther Hicks with a channel Esther brings through called Abraham.

I personally first tested manifestation on relationships. I made a list of everything I wanted from a partner. Right down to some minor details such as he must like lizards as I have a tattoo of a lizard on my back. The next date I went out on fitted the list perfectly, he even was wearing a ring with a lizard on it. I realized, however, that facts about a person, such as job, hobbies and interests, do not make up a person's vibe. The emotions are truly what we are looking for, and we can't bottle the secret to make those emotions happen. But we can manifest what we want to feel.

Many of the books on manifestation ask us to create the things that we want in our life thought the power of our thoughts. People are finding that this form of 'cosmic order' doesn't work for them. This is because the energy of our emotions is far more powerful.

We think we know what we want, but do we feel the same

way about it?

Some of the reasons we choose a cosmic order will be though social conditioning and perhaps not from what our heart desires. It maybe something that comes from a view of us based in childhood.

A client of mine called Charlotte told me she didn't believe in manifestation. She was just turning forty-one. She had always wanted a family and children, and at this point in her life she was in fear that it might never meet the right man to be the father of her children. I asked her to close her eyes and visualize herself with her husband and two small children. Charlotte smiled as she did this; I then told her they were shopping in a supermarket. Her face fell, I asked her how she felt now. "Terrified," she replied. Charlotte had come from a large family; she had seen her mother struggle. Although her hormones and her thoughts told her she wanted a family, the fear of becoming like her mother was blocking her meeting the man that would bring about a happy family.

Manifestation works on what we feel, not just what we think. The emotions give out a far stronger vibration. Healing what you have made your past mean to you, changing your mind and emotions about events, means that we can move through what we fear and move into a vibration of Love which is the strongest of the manifesting emotions.

When we understand what our emotions are we can link them to where they came from. Then learn to change our minds from the original thought that caused the emotion into a strong, positive thought, leading to a loving emotion. The universe isn't cruel enough to deliver what we order to allow us to blow it by not being able to handle it on an emotional level. You might look in a mirror and think "I have a strong, fit body" but if your reflection in the mirror isn't in alignment with these words, the emotion you may feel is one of sadness or despair. You might think "I am abundant and financially secure" but if the bills go unpaid, the fear emotion will be the stronger.

We can face our fears about our own success if we can connect and be honest about what those fears may be. You may want a family, but block the right energy to bring you the right partner by a fear of the expense of that family. You might want to be a famous TV presenter, but fear public ridicule.

The law of attraction works at its best when it comes to relationships. Not that there is extra power in the desire to find love over the desire for financial security but because relationships are one of the things in life you can't control and so we can't fix it with logic or planning. You already want the universe to bring you that relationship bliss. The reason you can't control it is because it involves another person's free will. With that in mind, never use manifestation to interfere with someone else's free will. Don't manifest on their behalf even if your intentions are for their greater good.

Personal story from Elouise

I have been through a number of fairly horrific relationships in my time and finally resolved to take responsibility for my destructive patterns. After a visit to the author of this book, I went away with a much higher self-esteem and some practical ways to attract a better kind of man. One of the points that stayed with me the most was the power of our thoughts to change the physical world. With this in mind, I set out the intention that I was going to meet a man that adored me and treated me like a princess. Gone were the days that I would endure being bet on over a game of pool (and lost), from now on I would only settle on respect and happiness.

Three weeks later I called NatWest to do a balance transfer and a friendly-sounding man answered. He asked if I was Ms, Mrs or Miss and when I said Ms, he asked if I was a spinster. I told him to f*ck off and we both laughed. We ended up chatting about the fact that I was transferring money for gig tickets and he admitted he was a musician. After half an hour he said that he had actually finished his shift but would love to talk another time. We swapped numbers and chatted for 5 hours every night for the next three days until I took the risk. I got on a train and went from London to Southampton to meet him and determine whether he was either the love of my life, or a troll with a sexy-sounding voice. Luckily it was the former and we have been together ever since. Less than a year later, he had moved to London and then later proposed overlooking the Grand Canyon. We are getting married in June on our two-year anniversary.

What makes this situation all the more amazing is that my fiancé should have finished work half an hour before he took my call and for some reason to stayed on. He had taken 70,000 calls in the time he had worked for the bank and only once gave his number out – to me. He is truly the nicest person I have ever met and has made me happier than I know possible. Every day he finds little ways to show me how much he loves me and in return my greatest desire is to make him smile. When I lie naked and wrapped around him, I feel utterly complete and more 'myself' than I have ever felt before. As long as we are together, wherever we stay feels like home. He was exactly what I asked the universe for and I feel very grateful that from setting the intention, he only took three weeks to meet from changing my viewpoint and being positive about love!

Attention and attraction

The law of attraction

For men and women the impulse of attraction is very different and unconscious. Men have millions of sperm and women one egg a month. Men are chasers and women are choosers. This is how our brains are hard-wired. Women who are male dominant in their energy may become the chasers and find they have little choice in the choosing. So what are women and men looking for in their attraction to a mate?

Like it or not, our attraction is based in the survival of the species. Even though we don't look at ourselves as being primal, we can see our society values beauty. Beauty and Sex appeal sells products to us on a very basic physical level. 'Nip and tuck' operations to make us look more attractive are now considered normal, with many people not hiding the fact they have had some work done. Modern surgery is becoming more and more advanced, making a world where the 'constant look of surprise' is no longer the cost of looking younger. Why would we put ourselves though so much just to be attractive? Surely we can't be so vain? We really haven't advanced so much in our attraction for the opposite sex; in fact we still initially go by the old primeval reactions to each other.

Large breasts have always been a sign of being able to feed the future generation.

Women put importance on how a man can earn an income that goes back to when men were hunter-gatherers. A man will look more for a woman's youthful physical appearance; a woman has a time frame attached to how long she will be able to have children due to the menopause, therefore men are often looking for younger-looking women to be able to carry their seed. Men don't experience this as they can father children much later into life.

According to the front page of the magazines, women find pectoral muscle very attractive. Pectoral muscles (or Pecs) really serve no purpose other than helping a man to pack a good punch. Going back to our roots, when villages could be pillaged, a woman would want the protection of a male around her. A man who could punch hard would be very handy and able to protect her and her children. However, evolutionary psychologist David Buss studied women from all over the world for five years. He discovered that from Aleut Eskimos to Americans, women are less concerned about physical appearance and more attracted to financial and material resources and social status. Of course this goes back yet again to the need to look after children.

Modern women in the search for equality have been more prone to allow their dopamine and testosterone to run away with them. Allowing them (with the help of contraception) to go to bed with a man a lot sooner than their foremothers. While a man can impregnate a woman and walk away, a woman is left with all of the consequences. Allowing men to do the chasing is good all round, and holding out before a woman has sex with a new partner can only be a good thing, providing a relationship is what she is looking for.

Flirting

Flirting isn't only used as a tool for getting a date, it sells! Flirting can seduce you into bed and seduce you into buying products you don't have a use for. It is a common language in our society. You might think you're no good at it for getting a date but we use it all the time in so many areas of our life; the person who is trying to get out of paying a fine for not having a valid train ticket may give a sorry smile and explain how stupid they are and how wonderful the conductor is; when we ask for directions we can put on the 'please help me' big doe-eyes. We also flirt to make other people feel good about themselves: "What a great haircut, it really suits you". For some people it is so much a part of their lives they really feel the loss of it if they become self-employed or start to work from home. They miss flirting with people at work. Flirting really makes a working day go quicker; the glint of humour in the eyes, the quick banter between colleagues. The person in a coffee shop who always tells you it's so great to see you, "you make my day when you walk into my shop".

The eyes are the windows to the soul, the more flirting you do with the eyes, the more you are making a soul to sex connection.

The eyes can express a cheeky sense of humour that says you will be fun in bed. They can smolder, taking time to move from the eyes of the person in front of you, down to your coffee cup and back again, with a slight bite of the lip and a smile. They can show a dirty side that says, "Watch out, I am a confident sexual predator!" For lessons on how to use your eyes to attract men, I would highly recommend going and seeing a burlesque dancer as far as you can... watch her eyes! You might think that this only works on men but without the need for fake eyelashes, make up and a glove between your teeth, men can give these looks in the same way women can. For women, why just see a burlesque performance you could take lessons yourself. Burlesque is a form of stripping which started in the 1840's. Normally involving more tease than removal of clothing, climaxing with an ending where breasts are shown but often with nipples covered. A burlesque class will be made up of women from all ages and sizes, most are not professional dancers; it's unlikely you will strip naked. These classes really help you grow in flirtatious confidence. A great teacher will show you, it's not in the moves, it's in the eyes. You might hold a feather boa out as if to flick it into someone's face in the audience (or in a lesson a row of empty chairs). Your eyes say "is it you? I like you, but no... You're cute but no, is it you, Oh yes it's you!" It is a great way to have fun and build confidence.

How to intuitively know when someone finds you sexually attractive

Attraction can hit us like a punch in the nose. It could be your server in a restaurant, your boss at work or a teacher at your child's school. It can leave you flustered for words, blushing, jabbering and unable to focus. If only the physical signs were always that obvious; some people react by not giving eye contact and avoiding the person. Our anxiety can grow when we feel out of control of our emotions, we may not see the logic that a twenty-one-year-old backpacker might not be the one – when you're a thirty-something and looking for the parent of your child-to-be, it's unlikely to be what you're really looking for but your body thinks it is! Attraction can turn a sane person mad wondering and interpreting every body movement and comment made. However, have you ever noticed how some people seem to have their own theme tune? In the same way as a television show will have a tune that gives you an idea of the kind of TV show it is; a situation comedy will have a bright upbeat sound, whereas a documentary may have a serious piece of classical music. People, if you know how to listen, have the same. Everything is made of vibration, so everything that exists in the world has different frequencies of vibration. Vibration is, of course, sound. Sounds we hear with our ears are interpreted by the brain into words or into a sound we recognize, such as the difference between car engine and a bus engine. We learn from our birth how to interpret what these different sounds mean and where they come from; any baby knows its mother's voice. We need these skills to protect ourselves. We can sense if a work colleague is in a bad mood before we even see their face, it's like the 'Vibe' they give off is a heavy vibration so we might feel that person is someone we want to avoid at that time. You might also notice that when you listen to someone's problems they say "I feel much lighter having talked to you"; you, however, may feel much heavier and indeed more tired. We may see this also in music; some makes us upbeat, others make us sad; this is because we unconsciously respond to the sounds all around us. As well as the sounds we hear from others it is often the sound we send out that gives them the impression of us, then they make a decision on if they are on the same frequency as us.

When someone finds us attractive, they send out a vibe. How we hear the sound people make without words is by feeling it in our body. You may call it a gut instinct or an inner knowing. How to get in touch with it is to put your hand on your heart and say these words in your head while looking at the person "Do you find me attractive?" You will then feel a sensation in the body that will feel joyous and light or heavy and sad. As far as possible don't analyze the feeling, as wishful thinking and insecurity will likely bog down the brain. For me as a young person I found interpreting the vibration of when someone found me attractive impossible to hear. I made the judgment most of the time that I wasn't attractive. They say youth is wasted on the young, I was wrong about that interpretation most of the time. If you don't see how fabulous you look, you don't hear when other people feel it. The judgment of how you see yourself means you don't see the possibility that is before you. I see many older women falling into the same trap again, thinking that most men are attracted only to younger women. Learning to listen to that inner part of yourself means you can overcome the judgments you lay on yourself and hear what others feel about you.

How the body gives away signs of attraction

When someone is attracted to you they will often mirror your movements, usually while retaining eye contact. This extra interest in you is normally a sign of attraction. They may also hold your gaze longer than is polite, or considered normal; maybe with rapid blinking, the pupils are often dilated and their eyebrow may arch. However, be warned! If you are talking about something that is personally interesting to them they will also pay you this kind of attention, especially if you are being complimentary. It can also be a sign that they have been trained to a stage three listener level like a therapist or life coach; most people listen to conversations at a stage one level, this involves them listening to what your saying for what will effect, or be about, them in some way. A good example of that is: "I read this great book about India" - "Oh, I've been to India". A stage two listener conversation might be: "I read this great book about India" - "Oh, really, what did it say? Why was it great?" At stage three when the first person says: "I read this great book about India", the listener is absorbing the whole person: body movements, tone of what is being said, looking for what's not being said and being completely engaged. It's easy to think this person sees you as being the centre of their universe. This is the kind of full attention we all crave.

So there are different reasons for it being given: because they are in love, or they are trained for this kind of absorbed listening, or they want you to love them and are profoundly insecure. The way to know the difference is through your intuition and to give this attention right back. If they shy away, it's likely they're coming from a non-Love place. If they match it...Hold on to your hat, you have a rare one!

Other signs you may see: playing with their hair or if they touch your hair at any time; this is defiantly a sexual movement. Any extra mouth movement; licking or biting lips; smiling a lot and puckering up of lips. Women may move shoulders back to allow the breasts to look fuller. Legs and feet pointing in your direction and leaning forward towards you are all positive signs. You might notice touching by accident, for example hands brushing each other when walking side by side, conversation speed will match your own, increased laughter and asking questions of a personal nature or asking your point of view on issues.

Humans pay more attention to the people they find attractive but attraction often has little to do with looks. I learned a valuable lesson while working on cruise ships; I was sitting with the male performers on the ship watching the girls dancing on the dance floor in the crew bar. These people had been hired to work on board the ship for how they looked and danced. I was enjoying being with all of these great-looking males and also felt privileged to be watching the girls looking over flirting with their eyes and moving seductively to be the centre of the male's attention. One of the guys turned to me and said, "Out of all of these girls on the dance floor, I would want to sleep with you the most." The brain attached to this 5'2" curvy body was confused. The group turned and looked, then there was a chorus of, "Me, too." When I asked why, they said, "Because you would be the best in bed." It was a simple comment, you might think not that complimentary, but it taught me that for a man, sexual attraction has little to do with looks and everything to do with style. That style is one that comes from your heart in the way you see life and are open to it.

Erotic dreams

Dreams can hold a great power over our waking day as well as our sleep.

Dreams that are vivid in color and content are often called Lucid. People can sometimes control lucid dreams; when they realize they are in a dream they can then decide how the dream unfolds. This means when a person has a dream of someone who has died and has full awareness of the fact they are dead but in the dream they act as if everything is normal about the two being together again. Another aspect of this is they can practice different sexual fantasies with perfect women and men as if they are experiencing the real thing. People may dream of meeting a celebrity or someone they have seen from television; dreaming of having sex with a celebrity is said to mean you are secretly a bit of an exhibitionist. It is also said that the spirit leaves the body and actually meets the person you are dreaming about. If in this lucid dreaming the two souls do meet it might mean that actors like Brad Pitt would have a very busy night's sleep!

The impact of erotic dreams can change the way you see the person you were dreaming about. Anyone who has dreamt that they are making love or even kissing someone that they have never previously found attractive can suddenly find himself or herself having a serious 'overnight' crush. This might be our higher guidance trying to tell us something, but it may show you are searching for an ideal lover. It can be quite alarming, especially if you're already in a relationship or the person dreamt about isn't available. It can also cause problems if the person is your boss, a friend, or even your friend's husband. The person in real life might still repulse you.

Dreams don't discriminate and it is hard to close a door to someone you may have fallen in love with in your sleep. You can have whole lifetimes in your dreams with this person that may make you feel unbalanced. Especially if you find yourself trawling the Internet trying to find information on an actor or actress you never even noticed before. Dreams of having sex with your boss or a person in power, like a policeman or woman, is giving you a sign that you want to take charge in bed or more power in your life.

The sex can also be far better and almost more vivid than anything we have experienced. This can cause us to feel aroused the whole next day about a person we don't know in our waking hours. Imagine if you see the person after the dream, you may have the same emotional response as if you made love to them in real life. You may blush, stammer and feel embarrassed and slightly ashamed of the night you spent, which they have no idea of. It is also a good opener for a chat up line, "I had a dream about you last night..."; anyone who has had one of these erotic dreams will understand what the seducer is hinting at.

Men may have an ejaculation (wet dream) and actually orgasm in their sleep. This doesn't even need to be a build-up of sexual desire. An ex-partner of mine had a wet dream while we were in bed together. In the dream he was flying over a field of topless milkmaids; I wonder which of the astral milkmaids got that one in the eye! Women can also wake up wet, but rarely (sadly) get to the orgasm stage in sleep without waking up.

When you have had one of these dreams try not to read too much into it. Have a look at the emotions involved and see where the dream maybe trying to tell you something. But try not to pitch your relationship hopes on "this is meant to be, as I dreamt it". Often a dream is playing out something from your subconscious mind for you to pay attention to. Try not to hold on to the message in the dream being literal, otherwise television actors would have a host of stalkers who say they are "the one" as they saw it in a dream!

Understanding your dreams

- Dreams are a part of our intuition. They may have the answers you need right now for your love life.
- Give the dream a film title. This will give you a way of connecting with the story.
- What was the main drama of the dream? Were you trying to get away from something? Are you being seduced or the seducer? How comfortable do you feel?
- Compare that in the dream to your real-life situation.

If you have problems remembering your dreams

- Whatever you remember, even if all you remember is a tiny piece, write it down; this trains your memory to remember more. Dreaming happens in the same part of our brain where short-term memory is stored so it's important to write it down before you forget.
- When you wake up after the dream, don't move from the position you woke up in. That's the position you were dreaming in. That will help you keep connected to the dream.
- Quiet your mind, and let the dream come back to you.

Removing blocks to finding a date

We are complex beings, we live in a universe dictated by our emotions and our emotions are the messengers of what we think and believe. Our intuition is our truth, but it is often hard to heed your intuition when your head is sending out many conflicting messages. In this section of the book we will look at what blocks us from finding a date and possible partner and explore the ways to eliminate those blocks.

Losing your virginity

I hate to call something as sacred as virginity a block, but to many, it can be a block to having sex. The reason is often a case of wanting to make sure you have chosen the right person. Wanting to wait for the right person, who ticks the "virginity boxes", takes time and there is lots of pressure. The boxes consist of:

- Someone you love or at least have deep feelings for.
- You need to know the person well and value them.
- This is the person you are likely to talk to your children about when you tell them the story of your first time. You will also tell your friends and people throughout your life when asked at drunken party games.
- You need to know the person will respect you, even if it all goes a bit wrong.
- You also need to make sure you can trust the situation to be safe with no unwanted pregnancy.

The teenage years are when most people lose their virginity. At this point in life it will be hard to find someone who matches the above criteria as someone for you to give the 'gift' to. Teenage boys seem to be blinded by hormones and will likely have a wonderful connection with the girl, only to then desire to practice their new found skill on other girls. Girls tend to be all full of self-doubt and insecurity and talk too much to their friends. Many of us will go for someone who fits most of, but not necessarily all of, the bill. We might get to a stage where peer pressure becomes too much. Many of us are told to "hold your virginity for the right person", but few of us are ever told that there will be people whom you will wish that you had slept with. Not necessarily the one that you wanted to lose your virginity to, as they weren't the right person, but someone with whom you would have had sex if you weren't a virgin. Those connections pass you by when you are waiting for your peer group to grow up emotionally.

The older you are as a virgin, the more pressure you feel yourself under; this is especially true for men. A man can take great pride in being the 'one' that a woman gives her gift to. There is then no other comparison for him and it gives him the chance to be the masculine force. For a sexually experienced woman it feels like a big responsibility to take the virginity of a man. If he has been waiting for the 'one' we know it must have been much harder for him to do this. So being 'the one' holds a great amount of emphasis. This woman may also fear he will want to run out into the world after and experiment with other women.

What I feel is important and valuable about losing your virginity is the circumstances. If you wait for the 'right' person, then the person you are looking for also seems to be the one you want to be with for many years to come. A sexual person will want to have had many experiences before they settle down. You don't buy a car without test-driving it first, but how do you know if the car is any good without having driven other cars? The more cars you drive the more you know what you want in a car. Also the more your driving skills improve, and you stop blaming the car for bad handling! If you catch my drift?

Someone who you are mad about, fancy like crazy but know you are not going to be with is perfectly fine to give your virginity to. You are the one that has to hold the memories of this special event. How would you like it to be? Even if it is a one-night stand, someone you meet on holiday and know you will never see again. The gift of giving your virginity is one you truly give to yourself. If you feel the situation is right, romantic and the kind of story you will tell in the future, go with how your body feels. Most people can take you back to two moments in history, the person and the day they wish they lost it, and the time they did.

I was working in a restaurant as a washer up I was 17. I finished my shift at 1:00am and decided to take my motorbike past the top of the road where the boy lived who I'd been thinking about all week, all summer, in fact all year. As I rounded the corner he was crossing the road with his dog (what are the chances!). We walked along the beach together and found a bench on a golf course. That was the moment, but I blew it because I thought I smelt of chip fat! Years later I was in a warm comfy bed with a man I knew and felt safe with and to this day I am still friends with. The beach is the night I think about most often, go with your passion, and never worry about the details (apart from condoms!).

If you have been without a partner *too long!*

You might not notice this happening, you might go through a busy work patch or just take a bit too long getting over your ex, but suddenly you realize that you have been single for ages!

You may have stopped finding people attractive, stopping masturbating, stopped even going out. In return suitable partners will have stopped looking at you because you've stopped sending out signals. Everything seems to stop, so you stop dressing up, or overdress out of desperation. The main thing to know is how to get started from stopped.

- Make time to masturbate!
- Read erotic fiction books
- Watch sexual films (this doesn't have to be porn)
- Dress sexy. This doesn't have to be stereotype sexy. I think a thin cotton blouse on a man or a woman is very sexy.
- Get a make over, new hair style, new clothes (use a personal shopper found in most department stores if you're unsure what even looks good anymore).

It really is a case of getting back into a habit. Take time to look at your life and start to make room for a relationship, even keeping a drawer empty in the bedroom. Lack of space in your life caused the drought, not you getting older, or fatter, or less funny. You just got consumed by things you found to be more important. Time to change your priorities!

You have secretly gone off the whole idea of relationships

It happens; you desperately want to be in a relationship, but the 'right' relationship. You have a list of what you don't want, based on the past bad experiences you have had. You doubt there is anyone nice and right for you in the world and deep inside you think you would be safer on your own. The list of disappointments overwhelms you and you just feel that it's not worth the risk. By the law of attraction you attract what you believe. You might think that you are sending out emotions of happiness and balance, those of a person who is easy-going and calm. But the rest of the world is being blasted with toxic dense vibes being sent out by your inner pain. Not all men are bastards and all women bitches. YOU CAN CONTROL HOW OTHER PEOPLE TREAT YOU! Realize this and go back to being open to trust. The point is the only person you need to trust is yourself. To trust yourself is to know you will walk away if you need to or voice an objection, take no crap and only be open to love. In your past 'bad' relationships I bet there was a moment when you knew, and I bet you ignored that moment and carried on without acting upon it. Make a promise to yourself that you will always act on your gut instincts and open your heart. Most women I have met who have been though a heart-crushing relationship, or even a series of them, can tell me of the moment they knew they should walk away and didn't. It can be when you first meet the person, or months or years into the relationship. I call it my "number 38 bus moment"; as the last time I stopped listening to it I was sitting on the number 38 bus, going to my boyfriend's place in Hackney, with him sitting beside me. My whole body wanted to get off that bus, but in that moment my mind said I was being stupid and it would hurt and upset him to just get up and leave without an explanation. If I had got off that bus in that moment I would have avoided a very painful time ahead.

Act upon your gut instincts; it's not very often that they are wrong. When you learn to trust yourself, you don't need to trust anyone else, and that means you can trust them because you trust *you* first.

When you can't get over your previous relationship

There is often an event in our life that impacts upon us so deeply we never really move on from it. Many people will tell you to 'get over it', but it's like a tattoo, it becomes a part of us and a part of our identity. Often this event in our life didn't even feel that significant at the time it was taking place, but the event just keeps coming up in our mind and we re-live that situation again and again.

Our past is no more real in our mind's memory than it is when recalling a dream. In fact it looks just like a dream when we view it in our mind's cinema screen. The way the image is played is exactly the same with color and textures as well our ability to forget bits and fill in the gaps. This is also how you visualize you would like your future to be then we even call it a 'dream'. The only thing that doesn't feel like a dream is the present moment in time, which can make us wonder if the past really did happen and if the future ever will. We mostly believe in the past because we can still recall the emotions. When this comes to relationships we can believe we are still in love. However, we can be in love in a dream with a man or woman we have never met and miss them in our waking hours. It's the decisions we have made on our perceptions of a situation that gives that situation its significance. So can we also dismiss our past as a dream and let it go in the same way? Certainly not as easily. Coming to terms with our past relationships and what they presented to us is what we all try and do, but some ex-lovers leave a stain on the soul that just won't shift. We can still think of a person we went to school with, or have more emotion for our ex of five years ago than for our current partner. Often when we can't get over someone we feel a sense of real grief. The same kind of grief as when someone dies, but with the added dimension that we feel we can't truly grieve if the person is still living. The grief we feel when someone dies is said to be a sadness caused by all of the things you wish you had said or done that never happened. We become sad about the future we will never have with them, we have a sense of failure and loss like we have lost an aspect of ourselves and can feel lost in the world. This grief has a very much stronger element but the long lasting emotions of grief at the end of a relationship can feel much the same.

We find it hardest to let go and move on from the memory of a relationship that caused us to least be like our real-true-selves. The situations where you didn't say what you wanted to, but also when you put on an act to please someone else or to keep the peace.

For example, how many times have you been in a hostile situation and afterwards gone over and over it, wishing you had said or done something different in reaction to it? Because Fear had crept in and said "I better not", or it overreacts and makes you say things out of character or honesty. Connection with our integrity and acting from the truth of who we are really is so important. Being in our truth and not in our ego is the only way to be; it means our relationships work, but also we don't have the nightmare of living in regret.

Often in a bad relationship we are working in order to try and turn the relationship around and make it better. We think if we love hard enough or long enough, if we don't say our needs and create who we think they want then they will stay. By creating this person we can often hide who we really are and swallow what we really want to say.

As children we often aren't able to say what we want and express ourselves, and our childhoods may contain unresolved issues we go back to and replay in our minds. We are not our fully-formed selves as children. We look back from our fully-formed selves at what we had wished we had done or understood better back then. We can't undo so we don't let go.

Relationships, situations and anything where we have left something unsaid, or anytime we weren't authentic, leaves an imprint of unfinished business we just can't seem to move on from. Undoing now is the key to letting go. The way to undo is through acceptance of you. Understanding the lesson, having gratitude for it and forgiving yourself. Not letting go can lead to dis-ease; not being at ease with who you are can lead to ill health. It is us who hurt at the end of the relationship if we weren't real. This means ideally being the real you with everyone you meet all the time.

Take a moment to list all the ex-partners you still haven't moved fully on from. As you look at each name, take a moment to think about who *you* were in the relationship rather than what they did or said to you. You might find they were reacting to a created you, not the real you, which is why the confusion and playing over the situations within the relationship still come up in your life today. Upon examination we can see when we were most at odds with ourselves and when we wanted acceptance from this particular person. By looking for acceptance from others when we don't fully love and accept ourselves, we, like the chameleon, adapt ourselves to blend in with our surroundings and the people within them. The best thing we can learn to do is talk from our heart and not from the ever-changing ego.

These kinds of relationships that confuse us the most and are often the ones we feel we must confess to our new partners. Within that confession somehow we are allowing a pattern to repeat. "This is how badly someone hurt me" becomes "This is how malleable I am and how much I will put up with", therefore giving permission for the same misconduct. The chances are in the new situation we will react in exactly the same way. The cry becomes "Why does this always happen to me?" The answer is: until we get present with the real self and stop trying to control how other people see us, we won't be in touch with our true-selves and therefore not in touch with what we are allowing. Speaking our truth from the heart and not through manipulation will help the shift. It will also mean we are free and don't replay and replay past relationships, wondering why he/she did this or that. Understanding this means we will know that the reason we can't understand our partners or what happened in the relationship is because they were reacting to a fake you. When we get real this misunderstanding just doesn't happen in relationships or any other situation in your life

Ways to let Love beat Fear

Love in its pure unconditional form is always transformative. Being mindful of what part of ourselves is communicating with the world, our ego or our love means we can make empowered decisions.

Next we look at how our own and society's fears can make or break how we find a date.

Don't believe all you hear about relationship statistics

We live in a society that revolves around fear. Our ego is fasci-nated with drama and bad news. Whatever our ego has an interest in sells and makes people money. We like to know of anything that might threaten the life that we have worked so hard at in order to provide for ourselves. Society as a whole believes there is a lack in the world and that we have to be very careful out there. The news and soap operas tell us so; the bad things we hear about people doing make it seem like there is no good news and all the good people are few and far between. We are taught to believe you have to be very lucky to find a good person, let alone a soulmate.

This isn't The Truth so don't make it Your Truth; there are wonderful people in the world but 'the wonderful people' find it hard to be so. There are too many tales of the do-gooder getting stabbed. With a world so linked in fear I'm surprised that love ever wins; but it does all the time. The trick is to break through this fear and get into our spirit self.

In our daily communication with each other we have a choice: on whether we communicate from the best of ourselves or from our fear-based ego-self and sound like the news we hear every day. Sometimes other people make it hard for us to be coming from our positive place or we fall into repeating bad news about the world that we hear. We then also project and see that to be possible in the people we meet every day. This can drive us into our defensive-self-protecting ego-states, which means we are not coming from our open loving self.

Most of our defensiveness or attacking in communication comes from the ego. Attack or be attacked! The ego is a part of our psyche, there to protect the physical body, to make sure we get food and a roof over our heads. The ego was most useful for cavemen, where they would have to fit in and manipulate the tribe in order not to get kicked out into the cold and die alone. Of course we are not in the cave any more so the ego-self must learn not to react in fear. It must also learn not to react when friends, family and the media talk about how bad relationships and people are; it needs to know that this isn't the truth for you and then your love will be profound.

The inner positive spin-doctor
We are all used to having negative thoughts and feelings from time to time. What we need to avoid is manifesting the things we don't want and losing the things we do. Not all of us get out of

bed looking forward to the day. However, if you can have the life in which you understand yourself, you'll wake up looking forward to the day with a new purpose. We can at any point transform our thoughts and feelings into being more positive and in return more powerful.

People who we are attracted to are often the people who seem to be having a joke inside their head that no one else can hear. They smile a lot. They don't get ruffled when others criticize them and we wonder what their secret is; they have a positive spin-doctor in their mind and you can have one too. A spin-doctor is used in politics to turn a bad political situation in to a good one for the press of the political party. Your life can be presented like a news broadcast.

"Today John Smith missed his train and narrowly made it into work on time. Critics say John Smith is showing signs of not being able to control his working day and are losing faith in his ability to be a successful human."

Alternatively:

"Today John Smith arrived bang on time for work despite having missed his train. Supporters say, 'this proves John Smith has capacity to run for the position of God in the next election.' I doubt any of us want to be God, but a successful human definitely!"

We fear criticism from others, but often give ourselves far worse.

We can spin the way we think and therefore feel about ourselves with a different perspective, turning the glass from half empty to half full.

The reason for doing this is to build faith in you. Without self-faith we don't take valuable steps towards a better life. Faith allows us to reach a little higher for the things we want. Faith allows us to love a little deeper. When we believe in ourselves we live without fear. This is achievable by changing how we interpret our day-to-day experiences. Were we fools who missed the train or amazing for still arriving on time even though we missed the train?

We have a choice for the life that we want to live. Our past doesn't have to dictate who we are today. Our future is not a predestined destination. In this very day we have the power to grow and change to become more wonderful and more powerful. The answer lies in our perception of ourselves.

How woman attack the one thing they really love... Men!

In your lifetime you are likely to hear many jokes about men and fewer jokes about women. It seems OK for television shows to male bash in a way that political correctness overlooks. I accept that in the previous generation, the reverse was true leading to the commonness of 'wife jokes', but today's male bashing isn't about humour, it's about criticism.

Here's an example of some of the male bashing stuff that arrives in my inbox:

For all those men who say, Why buy a cow when you can get milk for free. Here's an update for you: Nowadays, 80% of women are against marriage, WHY? Because women realize it's not worth buying an entire pig just to get a little sausage.

1. Men are like Laxatives. They irritate the crap out of you.
2. Men are like Bananas. The older they get, the less firm they are.
3. Men are like the Weather. Nothing can be done to change them.
4. Men are like Blenders you need One, but you're not quite sure why.
5. Men are like Chocolate Bars. Sweet, smooth, & they usually head right for your hips.
6. Men are like Commercials. You can't believe a word they say.
7. Men are like Department Stores ... Their clothes are always 1/2 off!

8. Men are like ... Government Bonds. They take soooooooo long to mature.

9. Men are like ... Mascara. They usually run at the first sign of emotion.

10. Men are like Popcorn. They satisfy you, but only for a little while.

11. Men are like Snowstorms. You never know when they're coming, how many inches you'll get or how long it will last.

12. Men are like Lava Lamps. Fun to look at but not very bright.

13. Men are like Parking Spots All the good ones are taken, the rest are handicapped.

Now send this to all the remarkable women you know, as well as to any understanding good-natured, fun kinda guys you might be lucky enough to know!!!!!!!!!!

Now re-read the list and think about how you would feel if someone was making these comments about you personally, or about your father, or Son, best friend or your new love.

I would like to change the last line:

Now send this to all the remarkable single women you know, to energetically scupper their chances of falling in love as they fear this stupid un-true stereotyping. As well as to any understanding good-natured, fun kinda guys who are trying to find their place in a new world of woman's liberation where they don't know if they should hold open doors anymore and why not cut off their balls energetically while you're at it. !!!!!!!!!!

Who writes this stuff? When will they stop and when will it all end up in the junk filter where it belongs? If you don't respect and admire the opposite sex, then by definition how can you respect your partner? Or even your children who are of the opposite sex? We really should never put each other down or give each other sexual stereotypes. The vibration that we are sending out when we do is a dense ugly vibration. You can imagine saying words like, "All men are bastards," and the effect that will have on your son or even your daughter. Like attracts like and if this energy of mistrust and hate toward the opposite sex in the form of male or female 'bashing' persists, then you are likely to attract into your life the very people you are expecting. We will say words like "Why are there no nice men?", but your belief will attract exactly the thing you are trying to avoid.

Patterns in relationships are very common. Often it's the belief and thought structure of the person with the pattern. If you change your mind you will draw to you different people. Just try thinking positive thoughts about the opposite sex for one week. Think of all of the wonderful qualities that exist, as if every man was like the matinee idols in the films. See if your experience changes.

Love is contagious, the more you send, the more it spreads. Sadly, so is anger! We have to fight this battle of the sexes by being positive of how we speak about each other and not allowing others to bash the sexes in our presence. This negative viewpoint has been going on for years and has done much damage to our relationship with each other.

Bring inner calm into your life

Have you ever noticed that if you are panicking, there is a part of you that is aware that you are panicking? Or if you are depressed there is a part or your mind aware that you are depressed? But have you also noticed that that awareness isn't depressed or panicked. Even if you have had too much to drink, there is a part of you that is aware that you are drunk. The part of you that is aware of you being drunk is completely sober.

Often we believe that the random thoughts in our head are

who we are, but we are not our thoughts. We might also think we are our emotions and that there is nothing we can do about our emotions; that we can't help how we feel, but we can. Because no matter how stressed at work we are, or how fearful about a situation there is also the part of ourselves who is the observer; that which is the awareness inside of ourselves. The awareness is always still. The awareness is always calm and of course sober. When we feel adverse emotions and would prefer a calmer aspect of ourselves to be running the show. We can take a moment to center ourselves and put the awareness-self in charge. We are not our thoughts; we are the thinker of our thoughts. We are not our emotions we are more than our emotions, we are even more than our body, which gives us the illusion that we are inside of it. Being in touch with the idea that we are so much more than these aspects of ourselves begins our freedom to be in charge of what we want to experience through our thoughts and emotions, without letting them rule our lives. If you have to give a public address in front of an audience of people, your stomach might be turning over, your palms sweating. Your throat could be dry. But your *awareness* of all of these undesired side effects of fear is completely calm and still. By listening to that part which is still, we calm the rest of the symptoms of fear down. So we become calm to the audience. That goes just as much for first dates or your wedding. You never have to feel the victim of your emotions when you know you are so much more than the emotions. Just put the part of you that is still and aware in charge.

Building more self-faith

Many of us feel that we would like to have more confidence. Confidence seems to be the key to dating success; however, too much confidence can also lead to our downfall. People sometimes mistrust a confident person, believing them to be putting on an act or they may come across as arrogant.

Confidence can also be knocked, however, self-faith can't.

Self-faith is an inner knowing; you don't know how you know something, you just do. For example I'm sure you feel that if you were in a train that becomes derailed, that you would help other people to safety if you were not hurt. Now unless you have been in a crisis of this kind, how would you know? You just know it inside of you. Yet when it comes to less important situations like social engagements, we might feel like we will say or do the wrong thing. If we have been hurt in the past due to relationships breaking down we look for assurances from a new partner so that we won't get hurt again. The truth is of course you never know what the future may bring. No one can promise not to hurt you. The key is to have faith in your own ability to cope and see it coming before it starts. When we hold a door open for another person we are in control of that door. When we allow someone to hold a door open for us, we have to trust that they won't let the door go in our face but, in addition to that, we need to know that we can trust ourselves to put out our hand and stop that door from breaking our nose. Our view of the world can be transformed by how we view ourselves in the form of how much faith we have in us. Faith is blind; it isn't based on past experience. You might never have been in a particular city in the world before, but you know you will find your way. Self-faith is the hope that we have. I have never felt truly prepared for any great undertaking in my life. I doubt you have, but you do it anyway.

REMEMBER even before you got out of bed this morning, you were perfect. Before you brushed your teeth or put on clean underwear or put a foot on the floor you were perfect.

There is nothing you need to achieve that will define who you are.

The definition of you is one of perfection without your having to lift a finger to make yourself perfect. We are used to looking at what we lack rather then celebrating who we are. Every morning is a fresh start for you to change your mind about yourself. When you look in the mirror you have the choice to see your eyes shining brightly, rather than looking for signs of aging. If we keep looking and defining ourselves by our achievements it will never feel like enough and in return, WE then don't feel like we are enough. If we don't feel like we are enough we might never feel quite ready for a relationship.

A person can only *Be* who they are and not *Do* who they are. To wake up this morning and be you with no need to be defined by what you do is already perfect.

Of course you cannot stay in bed and expect to be perfect all day. The world is out there waiting for you to shine your light into it. The world sees how wonderful you are and longs to be with you; to receive the love that you have to give, to be empowered by your strength and feel inspired by you. You can't keep that perfection to yourself any longer. Even if today you only walk down the street and smile at one person, you will be enough; if you did nothing but glow with the most positive impression of you that would be enough.

You know deep inside you have so much more to give, but nothing to prove.

We all want people to love us. But how many of us truly give that gift to ourselves? From being infants to playing at school with friends we learn that we need other people's love to survive. But we also need to love ourselves in much the same way. The idea of self-love can be lost in a sense of it being selfish; that you put yourself before others and are just out for what you can get. We often wouldn't treat our friends in the same way we treat and talk to ourselves. Self-respect is a strong root to start from. When we talk about ourselves disrespectfully we allow others to do the same. Even making comment about your physical appearance or saying things such as "silly me, or how stupid I am". You will soon find people catch on and will start talking to you and about you in the same manner. Try taking time for things that inspire you. Films or books, walks around a town or in the country can inspire us. Put work aside for your inspiration time and you will find your work will benefit from it. Love yourself through the food you eat, take time for meals rather than snacks. Your food is your source of power and energy; if you value what you put into your body, your body will work much better for you. Dance! Even if you feel you can't dance, move to music in some way even if it's just tapping your toe or fingers. You're celebrating your life-force and the passion running through you. You are unique; no one in the world is quite like you, and yet you can fit in with everybody if you choose to. You can overcome great adversity; you already have done this in your lifetime. You have the power to do remarkable things. Even a small woman can lift the weight of a car if there was a child in need of rescue. Not playing your part in life to the full doesn't serve with world. You have the opportunity to be a remarkable turning point in someone else's or even your own life. Your potential is massive. Loving yourself will serve that potential and help to bring it into being. It's amazing how when we love and honor ourselves our families, friends and work colleagues also do the same; when we doubt ourselves, others doubt us too.

Be the light in the world by shining your own light, inside and out.

Above all Don't Panic!

The longer you are single the more likely you are to gather evidence that you are never going to meet anyone. This evidence then plays on your mind and becomes a self-fulfilling prophecy. The most important thing is to be happy, even if it's happy being single, because happy single people don't stay single. Unhappy single ones do. No one wants to date a miserable person, even if you know you are only miserable because you are single. So even if you have to fake it until its true find something positive about your single life. Here are a few to start:

For every single person, there is someone who settled down too soon and regrets it.

The more people you meet and date the more you know yourself, what you want, and the more you appreciate the right person when you meet them.

Not likely to be wondering if the grass is greener.

As you are independent you are likely to have a relationship based on want rather than need.

The best sex is often with someone you don't love. It's unlikely you will do all of the kinky stuff with a life partner. So at least you can get all of that out of your system before you settle down.

So you have found your date, that's just the beginning...

Within those first few weeks of romance we look for signs, which can often hint at all sorts of complications. When we first meet there can be lust, hope, fear, insecurity, game-playing, and we are, hopefully, on our best behavior. Many of us hope that when we meet the right person we will just 'know' – some kind of intuition that tells us we have met someone who has a compatible frequency to us. Our personal theme tune is in harmony. For those of us who want to have a family, it is the single most important choice of our lives. We may not be looking to have a family, but we are still looking for a connection, a feeling that we are not on our own for no matter how long that connection may last.

Ways to control dating anxiety

Rather then controlling your anxiety by creating contact such as sending a text, checking your emails a thousand times or by making that call late at night, try these:

Breathe! Take a few deep breaths and relax your body on the out breath.

Get out of the house and go for a walk.

Find something to do to occupy your mind.

Play music and dance the tension out of your body

Call a friend and listen when they tell you to stop worrying about it and that they would be an idiot not to like you!

Trust that if something is meant to be it will be, and no amount of the illusion of doing the right thing or controlling it ever makes a wrong relationship right.

The early stage of a relationship is all about joy of meeting someone and falling in love. What you will tell your children and grandchildren is the story of your dating and what happened when you met. They won't want to hear about your sleepless nights wondering if this was the one and if they wanted you.

Observations when on a date

You can tell a lot about a person in the way they look. What a person is wearing, or the way they walk, take information from it as to who they are as a person. You can't help making your assumptions about a person, and often they are not wrong. For example if someone were wearing loose clothing and a pair of sneakers, I would say that this person likes to stay in and snuggle on the sofa rather than go out with friends. Looks, however, are often deceiving. A man who is into heavy metal music and takes his motorbike out every weekend can still wear a suit to work or even out on a date. Seeing past personal appearance by using your intuition is really important. Often in the later part of a relationship a couple will start to dress like each other's tastes. The joke of the wedding present of 'his and hers' matching towels is true when it becomes matching jumpers and jackets. Don't judge a book by its cover, as you are likely to re-cover it as soon as you get it home!

It's a good idea to be aware of the way you talk. A woman will be far more interested in a man who sounds like he is listening –

try using small phrases such as "yes, I see, go on". Women like to feel they are being understood on a deeper, more connected level. Men love flattery as much if not more than women. So don't feel that you are emasculating a man by telling him how great he looks. Telling a man what he is saying is interesting also makes him feel secure.

It helps on a date if you choose a venue with low lighting. In candlelight pupils dilate so you can see better, but when a person is feeling sexually aroused the pupils also dilate. Therefore a darker room adds to the sexual anticipation.

Often the colors people wear will tell you something about them. When a woman stands in front of the wardrobe and can't decide what to wear it's often because she feels insecure and is looking for the right color to put her at ease. When she feels confident she is happy to put on anything and will feel great in it.

Look for the colors people choose to wear. It doesn't always follow that this is a correct measure of a person, but it's a general idea of some of their characteristics.

Color chart

Color Indications

Red	Strong physical body and a well-grounded personality. A dynamic ambition, enthusiasm and passion, self-confidence and a strong sex drive.
Orange	Fun sociability and creativity. A person who is emotionally expressive, sensual, caring, confident and intelligent. Dark oranges suggest intimacy problems, lack of self-esteem.
Yellow	A lively, intelligent person. The ability to concentrate, to think logically, and to be self-motivated.
Green and Brown	The need for nature and wide-open spaces for this person. Light greens suggest a gentle nature that

is intuitive and caring.

Blue   This person can communicate truthfully and express creatively. Also has great compassion for others. Too much blue suggests feelings of sadness.

Purple   Strong spiritual awareness, sensitivity and commitment.

Black   Just goes with everything in your wardrobe!

Friends into lovers

We often have a feeling of anxiety when we meet someone who could be a potential partner. Not knowing what the other person thinks or feels about us can leave us feeling out of control. It's common to try and deal with that anxiety by rushing to the finished outcome of "do you have feelings for me?" before any feelings have had the time to develop. Women tend to decide what they think of someone much quicker than men, so a woman will often push to get a decision out of her man, but a woman will also change her mind quicker. Often when a man has decided how he feels, he fights to keep those feelings alive.

Look at dates as a way of developing a friendship rather than analyzing a potential relationship opportunity. The longer the relationship takes to become physical the deeper the bond you make. Once all the lust has died down (we discuss this in-depth in the next section of this book) a connection can be broken until a more loving emotion has also been established. Allow dating to take it's time and grow rather than rushing to the next stage.

When you have been friends with someone for a long time, you may wonder why you both get on so well, why you don't develop this friendship into a relationship. Personally I think it's a great idea. We worry that you can lose the friendship, and maybe you will, but if you find the person attractive and they feel the same about you, then there wasn't an honest friendship. When there is attraction it is hard to hear a friend talk about their new partner. If you don't find your friend attractive, don't attempt to start a relationship because you get on so well. The attraction often doesn't build and you can't walk away because there are so many feelings, just not all of the right ones. A relationship is a friend you want to sleep with, and have the intention of making that connection deeper.

Friends with benefits

This is a person that you find attractive and sleep with. You get on well as friends but you know this wouldn't work in a long-term relationship and hopefully they know it too. I say hopefully as some people are tempted to be in the sexual intimate comfort of one of these connections, but the other person is hoping they may one day fall in love with them and make this relationship exclusive. This, sadly, will rarely happen. Hope might make you think that the person just isn't in the right place for a commitment and that one day they will change their mind. If this was the right person for them, then nothing would get in the way of that developing all by itself. The link maybe attraction-only based; even though you like the person they may be too young or old for you at this time in your life. You may not have enough in common, or you know that an aspect in their personality would drive you crazy if you had to live with it. It could even be that they want; children, a dog, to leave the country, to join the Army, and you don't see this fitting into your life.

If there is the right balance between two people who are open about being 'shag buddies' then I personally think this is a good and healthy connection. It boosts your self-esteem, which makes you more attractive when you're more confident, and stops you having the overwhelming urge for sex that leads you to one night with the wrong kind of person. However, this can be a hard sexual connection to stop once you have met someone you really want to be with. The transition from someone familiar to someone unknown can be odd especially for women. This is worth keeping in mind, because at some point it will be time to say goodbye and one of you will feel the loss. It's a lottery to know which one it will be. Also it can be reassuring to know that if you ever become single again there is always one possibly still waiting in the wings.

Mixed messages

If you are receiving mixed messages from someone you find attractive and would like to or are dating, the chances are it will be being caused by mixed feelings. Not everyone knows what they want, some people take longer to find someone attractive, as what they find attractive in a person is complex. They may be not in the right place emotionally, for example, if the person is suffering from stress or is still grieving the end of a relationship. If you have good self-esteem you will be able to put yourself in the right position and know when it's time to give up and walk away.

Allow someone the time to notice that you find them attractive; if they are not giving you any time or positive interest signals, walk away. The chances are if they weren't sure about you they will be the minute you are no longer interested in them. If they weren't then that interest wasn't going to start to blossom with your perseverance, and if it had the relationship would've been unlikely to find a balance. See yourself as being fabulous and if someone else can't see that, then they are plain stupid. Don't fall into the trap of "but I really like him/her", you have to like yourself first and above all, then strangely other people do too!

What the ego wants in getting a date

The ego is like a self-understanding program. We don't really need that level of consciousness when we are making love, but the ego has planted demands in our society; so that if we don't orgasm, tie each other up and scream until the neighbors complain, we are doing it wrong and are inadequate, which keeps us away from the feeling of oneness that can be found in each other's arms.

Secretly we all believe that we are 'the one'. We believe we are somehow special; there is something about us that is different to other people. We want someone else to see it and feel that we are 'the one'. We are also looking for someone else that we can feel is 'the one', someone special that also see us to be special to him or her. The truth is we are all one, there is no duality.

As we have discovered, we are all an aspect of the one that split into smaller vibrational pieces at the time of the big bang. These pieces are all experiencing what they are not. Reconnecting with one of those divine pieces through open, loving sex, reminds us that we are not alone, that we were never separate from one another, and can lead us to that reminder that this is home. This is our nirvana, we just can't see it yet.

We all have a collective consciousness and we are all energy in vibration. Like I have said, you are not in your body; your body is inside of you. What you are is immortal; what you are is energy. We are looking for an energetic match, a vibe that is at one with our own.

We are spirit beings learning through experiences we are having in this physical existence. Many people who wish to develop their spiritual self-esteem look at sex as if it will get in the way of them reaching a level of enlightenment. Priests, nuns and monks take a vow of celibacy giving themselves instead to God. I disagree, for me the church and religion isn't the only way to 'get to God'. If we are all the creation of God, then we all have that energy inside of us. Through connection with another person's soul, through an intimate physical connection, we feel the presence of a divine energy. I'm not saying that God as a separate being comes into your bedroom, but that we are all in connection to that loving presence all the time. That creative loving God presence we all have inside of us, it knows it and living by it that is the key to happiness.

Most of the time we only want to be happy ourselves; when we are in love we want the happiness of another person. We move from an ego-self of wanting to be happy to our higher-self of wanting to give happiness. This can be the start of a bigger journey from "what about me" to "what about you".

We are living a physical experience for a reason. It is for our spirit's evolution, the part of us that lives on beyond death of the physical body. It is believed by many spiritual ambassadors that sex is linked with the ego and in order to transcend the ego you have to give up sex.

Sex can be linked to the ego when you use it as a way to simply 'get off' and make yourself happy. Ultimately that kind of sex becomes very dull and is short-lived. It doesn't make it wrong but you could be experiencing so much more. Even in a one-night stand you can give your full self to be shared with another person.

We have an ego because the ego keeps our physical body protected; it also fights hard for the survival of the species. It doesn't mean that we can't transcend the ego when it comes to making love to a person, even if it is our first sexual encounter with someone we hardly know. Their ego may bring about the idea of separation, but your love will bring about unity.

Ego-self = Separation
Higher-self = unity.

It's very much like having a split personality: the devil of the ego on one shoulder and the angel of the higher-self on the other. These are both voices in our head. We do have a choice about which thoughts we listen to. We are not our thoughts, but we are the 'thinker' of those thoughts. The thinker can teach the mind to have productive, positive thoughts, and you have a choice about which "head voice" you listen to.

Here are some perfect examples of the two:

Ego-self	Higher-self
If I have sex too quickly after meeting someone, the person will think I am easy.	I trust myself to let go and act when something feels right. I trust my partner not to put all sexual responsibility on my shoulders.
I haven't: shaved my legs, under my arms, shaved my face, plucked my eyebrows, cleaned my teeth etc; I can't let this person see me like this!	We are all human; we all have bodies. I trust my partner to not have unrealistic expectations.
If I make a move I might get rejected and then I'll be hurt.	No person can hurt me, we only hurt ourselves when our expectations don't turn out as we would like. I will release my expectations and give the compliment of telling another how attractive they are.

Our thoughts dictate what we make a situation or experience mean, and from that decision our emotions follow. Even if the decisions we made about a situation came from watching our parents when we are children. We do have a choice, to look at the root of our thoughts and to come from our higher-self. This raises our personal vibration. So in other words the sound that we send out into the world is a sound of Love and not of Fear.

This sound plays out from our energy field; like I have said: you are not in your body, but your body is inside of you. When you have sex with a person your energy fields intertwine, their song is joined with yours. There is no reason why you cannot read someone's energy and allow them to read yours, thus bringing forward the most amazing connection, both for long-term relationships and one-night stands.

People say *be yourself* when it comes to finding a relationship and as long as you can be comfortable with who you are this is good advice. But for the most part, many of us feel that if we are single we are lacking something, being yourself, therefore, then means being not enough to meet the person we long to meet. After all if we were enough we would be in the relationship and not have a string of perceived 'failed' liaisons behind us. I say be more than yourself! Because you are much more then you realize. You are made up of your body, your thoughts, your emotions and what you have made your past experiences mean to you. You are much more than your body or your thoughts, you are more than your emotions and you have a choice about how you view your past.

Body – If we all looked the same life would be dull. Often what we love about a person is all the quirks that make them unique.

Thoughts – If you think positively about yourself everyone else will too. If you see yourself as being an aspect of a divine force deserving of love and respect then that's what you will have in your life. You are the thinker of your thoughts. Get control of your fears and anxiety and be positive in all of your mind conversations.

Emotions – The common one: 'I'm scared of getting hurt'. We cannot truly love if we live in fear of its opposite counterpart. When we feel hurt we understand love. Don't have hurt as a measure of love; instead use laughter as its measure. When you think of love, don't think of pain; think of joy. What scares me more than feeling hurt is having no feelings at all. We recover from pain; we grow from it, it can bless our lives and bring us closer to our strength and our truth. Avoiding pain is an avoidance of life itself. Let's face it, life starts with an amount of physical pain. From the moment of our birth we feel pain then the immense power of the love from our mother. Emotions are our messengers telling us if we are on the right path. To avoid pain is to only hear half the message that the world is trying to give you with the greatest love in mind. This is the love for your spirit's growth and the evolution of your soul.

Your past – You might have witnessed your parent's relationship break down; you might have had a string of difficult relationships or met only people of the worst kind but I believe in the transformation of love and it can heal the perception you have had of your past.

What you are is a most amazing complex being with the capacity to create and transform your world. You have the ability to love and cherish as well as destroy the things you love most. You have free will and choice; you are a divine being and an aspect of God (whatever you feel God is to you). You are the God and Goddess rolled into one. You have limitless potential. When you shine that light others can't fail to notice it. When you see your light for yourself then you would never allow anyone to treat you with anything less than love and respect.

Fear in life is the greatest enemy. Fear has to it many aspects that cause us to create self-protection. Where there is Fear there is limitation and it is difficult for Love to grow. Without Fear, Love is limitless. The emotions we send out into the world we attract back, creating a life based on our perceptions: so if you send out Fear, in one of its many incarnations that it presents in your thoughts and emotions, you will attract it. No matter how Love represents itself it always transforms into being a positive force in your life. The Love you give out attracts more Love. Remain open to Love; find it in everything you look at and everything you do. Seek it out; every time you see lovers holding hands don't feel resentful of their happiness, see it as one more sign of what is around the corner for you.

Open your life and yourself to the idea that love is the greatest force and it will prove you right.

Part Two: Emotional Love

When we learn to trust our intuition we are in no doubt as to whether we can trust our relationship partner. So we can open more fully to Love and move away from Fear. We bond physically, as talked about previously, but also grow into expansion of self and explore safely without our fear of judgment as we can read our partner.

In simple terms being in a relationship presents you with an opportunity, an opportunity for self-discovery. It's interesting how we focus on understanding another human to see how well we fit together, but what we really learn is how we fit with the world. We see our plus points and our limitations through the eyes of another human, which give us the chance to see ourselves fully. We only know who we are when we can measure ourselves in comparison to someone else. We are looking for someone to compliment us, but we are also looking for challenge and growth. A relationship is the opportunity to have a deeper understanding of your sense of self. So while you are busy discovering this other person, witness yourself doing it. What judgments are you making, and what do they say about your own expansion of self and your consciousness of it?

This is an exciting time, full of possibility and expectation. You both watch each other as you circle each other's lives, remaining in full eye contact. The opportunities presented to you are life changing. Most of us fear change so we try as best as we can to hang on to aspects of our single life, before we fully venture into opening ourselves to the union. You don't have to open over night but the willingness, regardless of making your new partner jump through hoops to prove you can trust them, is the key. Being willing to open to love is also being willing to open to hurt.

This means you are entering this time without limits. It's the best you can hope for and it will inspire even the most nervous of partners to do the same. It also means that the early sexual experiences you share together will be open, connected and hopefully mind blowing. Closed, withheld sex is never great sex. Physical emotionless sex happens when you know a relationship is not going to work out, as there isn't a match, just a sexual attraction. This is experienced in what we have talked about in Part One of this book.

The next move

You change your status to say 'in a relationship' on Facebook and MySpace accounts and you have Twittered all about it (for those who have online social networks). You are in the process of introductions to friends and then family. You feel more alive as a person, aspects of yourself you didn't know existed come out; some of this is positive emotion and some perhaps a little based in fear. Whatever the flow of emotions you are going through you feel more colorful and the world feels more colorful. You can cope much better with the job you hated, and mundane tasks seem to skip by as your mind is elsewhere. The anticipation of discovering if this is 'the one' and looking for evidence of their emotions for you is the most exciting time of the relationship's growth, yet many people want to rush through this to know what happens in the end. You might not know what happens in the end for another fifty years, so, as far as you can, sit back and enjoy it and don't try to control your emotions or the person you are with. Anxiety over whether this is the 'right' relationship will only harm the build of the emotions. It's hard to feel anything when your attention is in your head thinking and analyzing.

There are one or two strange crunch points in a relationship so you will know if it is going to go the distance after some of these points have passed. The first is after about three months when the chemicals in the brain start to dull down and you get your logical rather than your emotional mind back. The next is at about six months when you deepen the relationship or start to long for the space of being single. At this time you also start to see flaws in your loved one and start to weight up if these things will drive you crazy as time goes on. If you make it past six months it is likely you will make it to two years unless something not based on the your partner's personality happens. At two years you start to plan if this is the one and if you do or don't want a family or any other future plans.

Contraception

Contraception is a large part of our sex lives. Why I include it is because we are complex beings; what we use is up to the individual but often this may lead to putting trust in things that only look at the physical body and not the whole picture of everything we are. I would like to open it up to discussion on a holistic level to give you something to think about.

We have had it drilled home that if you don't use a condom you can pass on or contract disease and infections, some of these infections you're not even safe from with a condom! Once in a longer-term relationship, and after a trip for a check up at the clinic, we might choose to take another form of contraception.

The world we live in has a strong pattern of cycles; the moon has a great impact on the earth's water by controlling the tides; we are made up of around 80% water, that means we are also influenced by the moon. Most women would menstruate at the full moon if they didn't interfere with their natural bodies. We interfere in many ways we don't even know about. For example we eat food out of season. Our body will store energy from food in the form of fat as we head towards winter to keep us warm and fed in times of lack, and realize energy as we head towards the heat of summer. The food we eat in season tells the body what time of year we are heading into. Give a mixed message from frozen or imported food and the body will store just in case. Many forms of contraception will interfere with a woman's menstruation cycle and hormones in the body.

- **The pill** contains estrogen and progesterone to suppress ovulation.
- **Contraceptive** implants slowly releases progesterone into your body.
- **The injection** contains progesterone.
- **The patch**, a bit like a nicotine patch, delivers estrogen and progesterone into the skin.

This is down to personal choice but the common sense facts are there. Your body is an amazingly complex divine living thing, yet we think we know better than it by messing with its natural cycles. This is a personal risk and maybe one you are happy to take; just keep in mind that we are more than our body, we are energy beings. One day I believe that we will look back on this time in medical history in the same way we do at medical history of the past, when they used to drill holes in people's heads to let out the demons that cause headaches. In the future we will wonder why people only treated the body and not the emotions as a combination, wondering why we took pills to heal a vibration misalignment.

Options for birth control are limited to the kinds that will interfere with how your body works naturally. Ones that go into the vagina and round the penis are not much better. Food or anything that goes into the mouth is under the strict testing of health laws; anything that goes into the vagina isn't under the same law and isn't tested in the same way.

The vagina can absorb through its walls, like the sperm that didn't reach the egg, in order to bring more nutrients into the body. This is why a woman can have toxic shock from using tampons due to a bacterial buildup which is then absorbed. There have also been worries raised about the production methods of tampons and it took years to address these concerns.

In the sexually-excited man, the penis picks up whatever hormones are released in the vagina by friction and osmosis while having sex. You may choose to use chemicals such as spermicide, lubricant, and fruit-flavored liquid sex aids but these will come under the same small level of testing as tampons and can be absorbed into the body.

Internal contraceptives are:

The diaphragm, a circular dome made of thin, soft latex (rubber) or silicone, and is inserted into the vagina before sex. A cap is similar but smaller.

Intrauterine device (IUD) or **intrauterine system (IUS)** is a small t-shaped device that prevents sperm from surviving in the cervix, womb or fallopian tubes either with copper or hormones.

My view is to respect your body. Use a contraception that works for you but look after yourself. The list of side effects on the box may only be the start of the picture. Although not perfect, for me the condom wins out over all.

What is 'falling in love'?

For the first few times a person has sex with a new partner there is a release of drug-like brain chemicals dopamine and serotonin. This is why most of us tell our friends "I've never felt like this before… No I mean it this time!" We feel amazing because of this person/love/lust all rolled into one. But Mother Nature has a cunning plan! Her aim is procreation of the species. She is unaware of contraception and she believes that if he hasn't got you pregnant in the two or three months in a relationship, the gentleman in question must be infertile and turns down this boost of chemicals, which leads a woman to think that he isn't Mr. Right after all. This makes it very difficult to trust or even hear your intuition for the first few months of a relationship. At this point listening to what your friends and family have to say holds importance unless they are all sad, single and jealous!

When a woman gives birth she feels 'romantic' love right away in the moment she first looks into her baby's eyes. MRI (magnetic resonance imaging) tests have been conducted which show that parts of the prefrontal cortex are turned off when men and woman are in love and when we love our children this means that we put up with the sleepless nights and all that having a new baby involves. If we didn't feel this love we might just walk away. It also explains why we watch our friends getting involved in relationships that seem so wrong from the outside; these areas of the brain are linked with feeling negative emotions and our ability to be able to assess the trustworthiness of others. Therefore it seems impossible to determine in a logical way whether someone is right for us, as we really are not thinking with the full use of our brain! We rush towards having sex with a new partner because our brains dumb down to encourage us to have children; this is also the case for same sex couples.

As long as we can keep that romantic love alive, we can put up with the socks on the floor, the seat on the toilet or whatever it is that annoys us. What helps build that love quickly is a life connection – if you like the same films, books, but also if you share a deep link like your background. For example if your father rejected you, and your partner's father rejected them, there is an "in common" feel for each other. Our emotions sing, telling us we are not the only one.

We use emotions to identify and describe how we are feeling at a given moment. We can logically make the distinction between the emotion and the feelings themselves. We will even feel them as sensations within the body, which we associate with particular emotional states. We learn which feeling in the body means which emotion during childhood. Often we perceive something to be good or bad, right or wrong by how pleasant or unpleasant the emotions feel. The symptoms of being excited are the same as being anxious. It depends if you perceive things as positive or negative. You will feel anxious before a roller coaster ride, or excited. The interpretation of the emotion depends on whether you like or dislike the adrenaline rush. This is the same as falling in love. Some people love the first feeling; others want to skip past this as fast as possible to know where the relationship is going so they feel safe.

When we identify a feeling, it then becomes an emotion. What has happened energetically is our perception of an event caused an energetic response in the emotional body. When this response is powerful enough it will be experienced as a physical sensation in the physical body due to the law of resonance. The body then produces chemical signals, which correspond to the emotion and these chemical signals carry the emotional energy into every cell in the body. This is what we do when we describe ourselves as falling in love. The event as described above could be fantastic fulfilling sex, or a mind-blowing orgasm. We might then mentally analyse this after the event and make a mental decision that we are not in love after all but in that very moment, with all of the chemicals in the body sending the message to every cell, we were.

There are many things that trigger an emotional loving response. Our mood will be determined not so much by what happens to us but by the way we *perceive* what happens to us, i.e. our thoughts and what we tell ourselves about our situation. In other words you can talk yourself into being in love by your perception of a situation. For example if your parents had a volatile relationship, you might perceive that 'make up' sex is the most loving.

The body itself will also affect our mood and emotions. Emotions are experienced in the body; fear may manifest itself as a sick feeling in the pit of the stomach and anger in the arms and legs. Sometimes we can change how we are feeling by adjusting breathing and posture. It is the combination of the body (posture, breath), mind (our thoughts, our beliefs) and spirit (our true-selves) that produce our emotional state of being in love.

Emotions are messages. They are a communication between our body and our spirit, with our mind as the mediator. Emotions may arise directly from the body, from past experiences, from our beliefs, from deep within what we call the subconscious. Your emotions are your guidance system through life; by responding to your emotions you can avoid damaging or painful relationships and sexual experience. Remembering mind rushing chemicals for the first three, or so, months.

Intuition, emotions, hormones and sexual desire

Our emotions but also our hormones heavily affect our sexual desires no matter what point in the relationship.

Surprisingly both women and men produce testosterone. Many of us think it's just men this hormone regulates the sex drive for. We often describe a highly sexed man as having too much testosterone. Women may produce more of this around the time of ovulation and feel more like having sex then. For some women this happens during the first week of their period when estrogen levels are increased. Both men and women's emotions are affected by their hormones; not the largely thought myth that it's just women around the time of their period.

A man's testosterone level can double in the morning. This can make him feel very sexy; however, testosterone can also make a man have mood swings between euphoria and depression. We often look for faults in our lives when we feel emotions we don't like, sometimes laying it at the feet of our partner if we are not experiencing the greatest sex drive. Our mild depression suddenly says a lot about the relationship, when the route of the problem may actually be hormonal.

A lack of sexual desire on a hormonal level can be caused by:
- Eczema
- Thyroid disorders

- Diabetes
- Depression
- Antibiotics and some cold and flu remedies.

It is viewed that men have a stronger sex drive then women. This isn't the case, sex drives between men and women are matched. Other factors play a large part: men can focus on one thing at a time; women tend to think of many things at once. The wrong thought for a woman such as "did I lock the back door" could drop the interest in sex, even during lovemaking.

Our emotions can be influenced by outside events. As we are energy beings we can also pick up the vibrational frequency sent out by another person's emotions. This is wonderful when the emotions are positive but if you have worked with someone experiencing a bad mood, that mood can rub off on you. Now you can see how this would have a bearing on you if you were in a relationship with someone going through a hard time, or someone having a destructive sexual fantasy while making love to you. Our emotions are more complex and easy to influence than you may have thought.

When we experience an emotion, we tend to do one of two things. One reaction is to *express* the emotion – to put it out there. We may feel that we are being *made* to feel a certain way by someone else, in which case we may have some kind of emotional outburst, often in the form of blame, self-pity, anger or recrimination. We may also *repress* the emotion; that is, ignore it and bottle it up, refusing to let it have any expression. This can lead to huge amounts of energy actually being stored in the body. The body eventually will register this energy as *"dis-ease"* with itself, possibly making us ill. All we can do is to try to honor and understand the emotion. Once we understand that it can be a message from our authentic-self, we can accept the message and understand why we are feeling a particular way. Once that understanding enters into our reality, a release immediately takes place.

Good, bad, right and wrong are perceptions. These are relative judgments, not absolutes. We sometimes make our lovers "bad" or " wrong" to make ourselves right for all kinds of reasons; sometimes destroying the relationship and the connection we have in order to suit the emotion we are having at the time. If we take responsibility for our emotions, we understand the message they give us might be about us and not our lover.

All emotions can be placed somewhere on a spectrum that has Love at one end and Fear at the other. Thoughts and feelings at the love end of the spectrum are of a high, light, positive vibration, while those at the fear end are of a lower vibration and will be dull, heavy, dense, and negative. Love is joyful, hopeful, trusting, and optimistic. Love brings you closer to the full experience of yourself and of life. Love joins us together, allowing us to see that we are all intimately connected. Fear is distrustful. Fear tells us lies. Fear separates and isolates us.

Building trust

Trust is deeply important for great sex. You might get a great sexual thrill from having sex with a person you hardly know but still your intuition will let you know if you are safe. Many times we have been with a partner we shouldn't have trusted; there was an aspect in us that knew this and we chose to ignore the warning signs.

Many things can break our trust for a lover, for example the refusal to use a condom, or doing something that they know you don't like. Without trust there really can be no sex.

There is a chemical, which is realized in the body when we trust people, called oxytocin. It is found at its highest level when a woman is breast-feeding; it bonds the mother to the child. Rewarding activities also release this hormone such as eating, touching and warm baths. It is also released when we have an orgasm, which makes up part of the beautiful afterglow feeling when everything feels wonderful in the world.

A nice position to help a build trust is for the man or the woman to sit in-between their partner's legs, facing forwards and leaning back against their partner's chest. They are then being hugged as the partner reaches round and massages the penis or vagina – a very relaxing way to reach orgasm.

A woman's ability to reach an orgasm depends largely on how comfortable she is; it doesn't take much to make many women feel uncomfortable enough not to reach orgasm. A difficult conversation before lovemaking with her partner or someone else, bad breath, stress at work, a knee in the wrong place can, in some cases, cut sexual interest altogether. For a woman the desire for sex depends on what happens to her twenty-four hours before sex; for a man it's three minutes. Bad past events can also occupy a woman's mind, which will stop her building to orgasm. Feelings of lack of safety or shame can be triggers. A friend of mine who had an abortion found it difficult to have an orgasm for up to two years after. Also women who work hard with a multitasking lifestyle will find there are too many distractions for her to focus on making love. Some things will be harder to escape than others; going on holiday may be a great idea to reduce the stress of life and focus on the build up for great sex.

Intuitive Intimacy

The more you are aware of your partner the more you will build trust, listening to their body with the whole of your being and energy. I'm sure you have experienced situations where the person you are having sex with is actually hurting you, you move your body out of the way to make them stop and they chase you across the bed to continue as if you are moving away from the intense ecstasy of their hard rubbing! This is become they have become focused on their own experience and not the shared experience of lovemaking.

At the point of orgasm how many of us still feel connected to our partner? Probably not many, most people are thinking about the sensation, a fantasy, the relationship or even sometimes someone else to be able to orgasm. Try keeping your eyes open, focused on the present and look directly into your lover's eyes as you orgasm, a very difficult thing to do. Allowing someone to look into your soul at that moment opens up a unique connection. If you can keep your anxiety about being so open at a reasonable level you will get more intimacy. That intimacy brings growth of the relationship and of the self. Many women want to be present in the moment with that man they are with but then find it difficult to orgasm because they think they risk loosing the intimacy for the orgasm. I say it's possible to do both by managing our nerves. We can do this; most of us managed our nerves with our first kiss.

The anxiety may come for many reasons. Most of us believe if he knew this or that about me, he wouldn't love me, so we hide things on many levels. While sleeping in spoons position, how many women stop a lover putting their hand on their tummy by taking the hand and holding it away? I know most of my friends have, including the skinny ones! What would be the worst that would happen if your lover were truly touching your real body? He may not like it...and therefore not like you. Do we really believe he doesn't know? But he still shares our body and our bed space. Maybe we need to credit our lovers with a bit more than that!

Bob Niemerow of nourishthrutouch.com shares his story on how to build Intuitive Intimacy:

Over the course of my life, there have only been a handful of things that has genuinely affected me on a day-to-day basis. One of those occurred when I showed up for a weekend course 25 years ago called Basic Sensuality. One small part of that course, to me, was quite revolutionary. They put forth the proposition that the way to have someone feel best when I am touching them is to touch for my own pleasure.

Huh?! "Isn't that selfish?" I thought. They went on to say that when we touch someone, to touch as though we were running our hand over the softest fur. When we do that, we are paying attention to the pleasurable sensations in our hand, not trying to make the fur feel good. The optimal way to pleasure some one, it turns out, is to touch them for our pleasure.

Perhaps this seems counter-intuitive. Shouldn't we be trying to "make" them feel good, even if it doesn't feel particularly good to us? Isn't that part of being a "good lover"? While learning touching or sexual techniques may produce pleasure and orgasms in your partner, there is a much more fundamental skill that will revolutionize the way you touch.

Our homework assignment that night was to go home with our partner and do a touch exercise. I was to run my hand over her body and notice if certain areas felt better to me, then ask if that area felt better to her. When I found an area that felt particularly good, I was to keep rubbing there and notice if my pleasurable sensations changed. Did it start to feel better, stay the same, or start to feel not as good as it just had? When a change in my sensation occurred, I was to ask her if she just experienced the same change in sensation.

"Oh my god!" I could tell where it felt best to her by what felt best to me. Not only that, I could know whether it was feeling better, worse or the same to her if I was having that experience in my body!! Wow! This was really cool!! And it didn't matter if I was touching her arm or her clitoris. I could know moment to moment in the most nuanced way how my touch was feeling to her. It was like we were empaths. All I had to do was tune into my own experience.

After several times of practicing this with my partner, I came to be quite confident in my newly learned skill. I saw that this was a highly accurate (although not foolproof) way of being connected into my partner's felt experience. If at any time I were unsure about my partner's experience of my touch, I would simply ask her.

This radically changed the way that I touched and made love. I was far less concerned if I was doing it "right". My hands became like "pleasure hounds", seeking out the most delicious sensations they could find. And when the pleasure began to wane, they would start off again, following their impulse- looking for other exquisitely pleasurable sensations. Moreover, I found that this worked touching with any part of our bodies. What this did is transform touching and lovemaking from something we did "to" each other, to a shared tactile dance. I was able to read what felt good to her and know when it was not so pleasurable and time to move on.

But wait, there's more! By paying attention to my internal sense of my partner, I could tell if she was being fully attentive to my touch or if her attention was on some thoughts in her head. I also discovered that if I was losing interest in touching a certain way, she was also having the same experience. We were mirroring each other's experience.

Telepathy – Feeling at a distance

We can build intimacy by using telepathy. This isn't the commonly held idea of being able to hear thoughts. Many people think that telepathy is being able to literally hear the words in another person's mind. This concept of telepathy as mind-reading in the way that TV and films often portray it is, in fact, a misconception, and most people are to some degree telepathic. However, anyone expecting to hear somebody else's voice in their head may never notice the ways in which they are already telepathic. The word telepathy means 'feeling at a distance', which is a brilliant description for it. It is the ability to tune in to the feelings of another; Many times we know how a person is feeling without having to ask but before we take the time to refine our feeling-sense of what the situation is with them, we just come out and ask, 'are you OK?' We are most comfortable communicating verbally as it is the most sophisticated means of communication at our disposal and is least likely to be misinterpreted. Yet even so, when we communicate with one another most of the information being exchanged is non-verbal and some of it is non-physical. The level at which we communicate involving non-verbal and non-physical information exchange is beyond the range of all other five-sensory detectors and could be described as picking up vibes from people, which then get translated by our own minds back into thoughts, words and images so that our higher-mind can quickly and easily obtain the relevant information and move on. It is not at all uncommon for people in a close relationship to communicate telepathically with one another, literally sharing thoughts and saying the same thing at the same time to the point of it being difficult to say which person thought of something first.

So how does telepathy work? Imagine a mother who is skilled at sending a "don't you DARE" vibe to her son, which is handy for keeping him in check in social situations. The mother's *don't-you-dare* thought is accompanied by a strong don't-you dare feeling, which is then sent in a concentrated form to the son by the strength of her intention to communicate. This is literally how we put feeling into words. The son experiences a very clear signal from the mother in response to his actions and probably doesn't dare. The important thing to notice is that below the level of the verbalized thought "Don't you dare" the thought exists on a pre-verbalized level – a *vibrational* level. There is a don't-you-dare feeling vibration, which attracts from your mind the words that are in closest vibrational alignment with the feeling behind the words. Most of us think our thoughts *are* the words inside our heads, but the words themselves are just the tip of the iceberg in terms of the thought in its totality as a vibrational entity in its own right. Imagine you are in conversation and someone asks you a question to which you feel you have an answer. What happens is you open your mouth, confident that the answer will flow, despite the fact that most of us at that moment have not given thought to which words we will be using in our reply. Yet we are aware that we have an answer, to which we add the appropriate words as we go, almost as if the thought itself is searching our vocabulary for the best fitting words. To understand telepathy, you must understand that it is this pre-verbalized vibrational state of the thought that is being transmitted and received. To strengthen this ability we need only to amplify the signals when we are sending, which takes only breath and intention, and to be more receptive receivers, which means the ability to read these subtle feeling-fluctuations and being able to recognize when these are in response to the energy of another. The Bushmen of the Kalahari describe this close connection as being like having a telegraph located in the chest. When the men are out hunting, they may be gone for days at a time, yet the very moment they make a successful kill, the women in the village know immediately and begin to joyfully prepare for the imminent feast. You can telepathically know when your partner is close to orgasm or where they want to be touched and how. We can even tune into and have the same fantasy and feelings at the same time.

Exercise: Strengthening Non-Verbal, Non-Physical Communication

This is an exercise that can be done in pairs. You will need: a blindfold, a large floor space, and some furniture to use as obstacles. One person wears the blindfold and is guided to walk round the obstacles using words such as 'left, right, stop,' etc.

For the second time round the obstacles are moved and now the only form of communication is through sound without words, the person in the blindfold must feel the intention behind these sounds, of course more difficult when it comes to left and right.

With the third round the obstacles are moved yet again. This time the person giving the directions must only do so by sending feelings. The person in the blindfold must be open to sense what is being conveyed to them. Mark down your results and keep trying this until you get it right.

In the same way we did the above exercise, it is also possible to follow someone's energy field. You can do this with one person wearing the blindfold, while the other walks in front of them backwards, holding their hands out towards the person in the blindfold. You can then follow the energy coming from the palms of the hands; the palms of the hands have mini chakra points in them, which can send and receive lots of energy use your breath to direct your energy. Play with how much and how little energy you are sending; it can be felt by tingling in the hands or heat. This is one of the ways 'hands-on healing' is done, by sending out *healing energy* and *intention* through the hands.

Using telepathy through masturbation to keep connection when apart from your lover

There is nothing worse when you have just got together with someone than then having to be apart. Couples may often masturbate and think about each other during lovemaking and they feel connected that way, but it is possible to exchange energy between you both no matter how far the distance. If you both arrange a time to masturbate and focus your attention on each other you can really feel each other's presence almost as if you are in the same room. This can be very useful for long distance relationships. Remember to remain connected to them during your afterglow, it is at this point that the most amount of loving energy can be sent. Feeling all snugly can really feel like the person is in the bed next to you. Intention is very powerful and our energy systems can be in many places at once.

Giving meditation time to lovemaking

Our lives are often a rushed stressful blur of earning a living, looking after children, being social and all of the things we try and fit into a limited time. We often don't make to time for our partners or even for our own meditation and time alone. Here are some ways that you can blend meditation with lovemaking. The art of meditation is to keep the mind clear and unfocused on any thoughts. Thoughts may come in and pass through the mind, but not be hung onto. Making love in this way means it becomes a blurred off focus connection with the body, emotions and spirit, the mind and thoughts are put to the background. Start off with a hot bath or shower to allow each other time to have a moment to yourselves before you begin, just to let go of the working day or to check in with yourself. Make the lighting soft by using candles or low lighting. Check the room temperature is comfortable without clothes on (warm feet are very important). Play music that won't be too distracting; the idea is to create an atmosphere that will bring about a deep level of erotic relaxation.

Exploring with sexual touch as Bob Niemerow explained earlier is subtle, powerful and incredibly intimate. Try and be free of any self-consciousness, asking your partner being touched to wear a blindfold may free you up to move and touch in ways that might feel awkward if you were being watched. Start with the feet and work your way up if you feel uninspired to know where to start. Don't be critical of your partner's body; if these thoughts come into your head let them go and replace them with love. Know that these thoughts come from your own insecurity and have little to do with your partner's perfections or imperfections. See your partner as a wonderful work of art. Use conversation; your partner might be feeling a little self-conscious and saying words like: I love the way your hip curves, or your hair falls on your cheek will act as a positive affirmation. Notice both your partner's reactions to your touch and how it feels to you. Pay attention to any noises they make, watch for changes in their facial expression. Don't forget different kinds of touch: rub, scratch, tickle, firm and commanding, soft and gentle. As you are touching your partner visualize energy flowing out of your body and into your partner's body via the touching.

Be focused in the moment; if your mind starts to wander bring yourself back to it.

We are often around a person but rarely 'with' them. By taking the time to be conscious about being with them, we can see so much more than we thought was there. The depth of our connections relies on our willingness to be open and our availability to that openness. We often think being open is about being open in what we are saying but it is also about making our soul available for connection.

For those of you wishing to develop intuitive touch on a deeper level and use it for healing, I recommend studying Marion Rosen's 'Rosen method'. Rosen Method is gentle direct touch, using hands that intuitively listen to the body rather than manipulate.

Being mindful of our thoughts

Sometimes when we have had a stressful day, or if we are not really up for sex – but feel we should! – we can fall back on sexual fantasies that we know will bring us into sexual focus quicker. Our imaginative fantasies maybe the opposite of what we would like to experience in real life, we might not want to look at our love-partner in that way or even want them to act like that. We may be focused on another fantasy lover and not the person we are with. Through the law of attraction we understand that our thoughts and emotions bring to us what we are thinking about (check out Jerry and Esther Hicks *The Law of Attraction*) that doesn't mean that you can use manifestation to bring into your life one person you have your eye on, or change your partner's behavior. Your thoughts and emotions create your future unless you are in conflict with someone else's free will. So as our mind is a magnet and we can attract what we think about, be aware of your sexual fantasies. The man you feel turned on by might not be kind of man you want in your relationship so avoid giving out mixed messages. Recognize where your fantasies come from; for example a woman who has to be very much in control in her job might fantasize about being out of control in the bedroom. Sexual role-play is great fun; make your fantasies be about role-play and not about reality.

A test was done where a man sent positive thoughts to his girlfriend all day, that night they had a great connection and had wonderful sex. The next day he was annoyed with her and although he never mentioned it, his girlfriend was frosty with him. Your thoughts have an impact when you think about a person. I have tried this with a noisy neighbor. When I was angry at her for one disturbed night's sleep it got worse; when I didn't emotionally react I could tell she was making more effort when closing the door. If you fantasize about a person or situation make it positive or at least give it an ending with a hug.

The Physical Body
This is an anatomy section you might not feel you need, after all this is a book on sexual intuition. However 'mind, body and spirit' are connected. It is impossible to fully understand one without the others.

The physical body should be vaguely familiar to us all, and most people these days have a basic awareness of their anatomy and physiology, information on how to look after themselves through diet and exercise is widely available. There are many overlapping systems in operation within the body. There is your skeletal system, which provides your physical shape, the muscle system that makes motion possible. There is your blood system which keeps all parts of your body supplied with oxygen from your respiratory system and bio-organic fuel from your digestive system, and disposes of toxins in the form of carbon dioxide that is then released when you exhale and other fairly obvious ways of getting waste material from the inside to the outside. You have an immune system working to neutralize and eliminate any toxic elements that get in, an endocrine system, which carefully generates and releases chemicals into the body to alter its state, and is itself closely linked to the emotions. You have a complex sensory system by which you take in information about the world around you. Assuming full health and ability, you have sight which allows you to take in light energy and turn it into clear, immediate and detailed information about your surroundings. Your sense of touch gives you detailed feedback about the objects that you come into contact with. Our sense of hearing allows us to detect sound energy, while taste and smell allow you to distinguish between thousands upon millions of chemical signals. You have the nervous system controlling and monitoring all these bodily systems all wired up to the central computer – the brain – which works according to the natural principals of life to maintain and preserve life. It therefore automatically takes charge of all the body's many jobs and organizes everything at a cellular and energetic level. To a large degree it is self-repairing and self-maintaining (provided we don't accidentally reprogram it) leaving you free to get on with whatever it is you choose to do with your life.

Connecting Body and Soul

When you connect your consciousness and awareness to your body, your soul flows there too. Just through your mindful intention you can put your soul into any part of your body. I was once told that the soul is the size of your thumb; I don't feel that to be true, but imagine for a moment if it was. You could put it anywhere! When we focus our attention onto an aspect of our body our energy follows. That part of our body becomes intuitive, it can feel, hear, know, absorb and give energy. As we go through the sections of the body, imagining the power you would give each part if your intuition, emotion and very soul were connecting purely from that area.

Soul Kissing

Kissing is one sexual act acceptable to do in public. It is the loving expression we show the world, even if people do tell you to 'get a room!'

A kiss doesn't start with your lips; it starts with your eyes. The eyes are to gateway to your soul, and it's your soul that makes the connection to start the kiss. The lips are the gateway to the genitals; a kiss done well will lead very quickly to a flushing of blood and tightening of the muscles in the penis and vagina, and it feels ecstatic! Hold eye contact and maybe even place a hand on the face or neck. Allow the start of a kiss to be tender and soft, lips only exploring before lust depends the kiss to move faster and become impassioned with tongues. Of course each kiss will have its own set of circumstances. The kiss that shouldn't be or has been a very long time coming is likely to be passionate from the offset, pulling and pushing as you tug at each other for more contact, so much so that a passerby might think you are eating each other. Let's face it, being pinned up against a wall and kissed hard by someone you are desperate to kiss is a real turn-on and the stuff of fantasy and film.

Clitoris connection and female orgasm

The clitoris has 8,000 nerve endings, twice as many as the penis; it's a wonder why there is so much difficulty and discussion about the female orgasm. The purpose of the female orgasm is to suck sperm into the cervix bringing it up closer to the egg. This is why it takes a woman longer to climax than a man. MRI scans have shown that the part of the brain that governs emotional feelings such as fear and anxiety switch off when a woman is having an orgasm. So the female orgasm is about letting go or releasing. The male brain becomes more active.

For my personal belief, I believe that the female orgasm starts in the right-hand side of the brain. The right-hand side of the brain perceives in whole pictures, it is also the feminine half of the brain. The left-hand male side of the brain perceives in parts. So the right-hand side of the brain would see a motorbike as a whole, the left would see it in parts, such as the engine size, the CC, what make and model. A woman could tell you what color the motorbike was. This isn't true of all women and men; I have seen some left-brain women and right-brain men.

As the female sexual experience will be in the right-hand side of the brain, it is experienced as a whole. That's one of the reasons why foreplay is so important, because there is more going on in the mind than the sex that's taking place. It takes time for the female right-brain to become focused on the experience.

When a man goes down on a woman she may be thinking all sorts of things but if he is really enjoying himself she is less likely to have thoughts that will stop her having an orgasm. The trick is for the man to take his time; the more time a man takes the faster she will orgasm. For most women soft gentle strokes work best, but that isn't to say that women only like soft loving sex, lustful sex is also wonderful for many women, but the clitoris responds better with a lighter touch.

The clitoris needs to be hard to be able to achieve orgasm. Ways of bringing on a female hard on is:

- The woman can clench and relax the clitoris muscles in a form of pulsing contraction as the clit is being stimulated.

- Soft strokes with the fingers circling round, hard brushing can lose the hard on.
- Licking rhythmically which is great to pulse your clit in time with.
- Slapping the area, but might be an idea to check with your partner. A good slap will bring blood rushing to the area.

Many women can be detached during sex, able to play porn star characters or be able to be in a fantasy state, but to reach orgasm she often needs to feel connected to someone. It is after an orgasm that a woman will allow herself to truly be loved. Just after the peak of the orgasm a woman will let out a different kind of breath. This one comes from her stomach area just below the bellybutton where the sacral chakra is situated. This breath is a release of anything stored in a sacral area, which is negative. The sacral chakra is linked to our emotional self, this release of breath is a letting go of any pent-up negative emotion which gets stored. This can also explain why when a woman is stressed someone might say 'she needs to get laid'. What she really needs is a good hard orgasm that shifts whatever she is holding on to. Not the nicest of breaths for your lover to breath in, but won't do them any harm. A woman may find that the taste in the back of the mouth will change; it's the kind of taste you have first thing in the morning, but you're likely to be too blissed out to notice!

One of the best ways for a woman to reach an internal orgasm is by entering the vagina with the penis shallowly for a few bursts and then deep for one; this is because you are stimulating the elusive G-spot. Only 20% of the female population have penetration orgasms and many women find that the vagina loses sensitivity with deep penetrative sex done in a kind of 'banging away' fashion. Orgasms reached during deep penetration come when the women is really turned on, and the clit is often involved even if it's just by body to body moment and not direct stimulation. The G-spot is found most easily by your partner inserting their middle finger, palm up, into your vagina and curling their finger. This fleshy mound is it. This area is the female prostate gland. The male prostate gland is in the anus. Both the male and the female prostate become wetter when stimulated. Through massaging this area is it also possible to bring on a female ejaculation orgasm. Fingering is the best way to stimulate a G-spot orgasm as I personally feel that it just isn't sensitive enough to a penis, after all you have to pass a baby through that area.

Female ejaculation; this is Claire's experience:

I have ejaculated for years and worried that it was a sign of a weak bladder but it smelt different and had a different texture; I could find nothing about it in books, until I found a brief referral to it. No more than about four lines. Once I realized I wasn't just 'wetting myself' as one partner insisted, I had to know more, I had to understand it. With the information that is now on the web it's made it much easier; researchers say it does come from the urethra but is produced by the tissue that makes up the G-spot. I ejaculate when I'm having a G-spot orgasm. It is very similar in chemical make-up to the stuff sperm swims in. For some people it's just a trickle but for me it's most often a flood.

It is also possible for you to tune into your partner's sexual experience and feel their orgasm in your own body, but without the peak. If we can tune in when a person is feeling sad and feel that that person feels, then we can feel another's orgasm. This is wonderful when you realize that you can even bring about your own full orgasm while experiencing your partner's and when you get really good at it you are not sure which one of you it is that's 'cumming'. The best way to do this is to visualize your energy with your lover blending. See yourself as being at one with them, that their movement is your movement. The more you practice this the more connection you will feel. What this feels like will be different from couple to couple, often it is a warm glow of vibrational energy you can feel intertwining both of you.

The Penis

The Penis is 5 to 7 inches when erect. The average female vagina is 4 inches, so let's make an important point about penis size. A long cock will be banging out Morse code on a cervix can hurt. For a woman it's not the length it is the girth that counts! As the width of the penis will mean it will rub against the G-spot. If the penis has a bulbous end, even better!

The head of the cock has more nerve endings in it than anywhere else of the penis; also tensing vaginal muscles at the same time as pulsing the clitoris (as described above) can be wonderful for both parties. When a man has oral sex the best part to focus licking is the fraenulum, which is a long strip of skin running from the head to the underside of the penis. Looks a little bit like the underside of your tongue. Don't be afraid of eye contact during oral sex, men tend to be very visual; as they are in the left brain they will be very focused on the experience that they are having. Looking up and into their eyes is hugely arousing for some men. It keeps the connection between both of you and makes the act of a blow job loving rather than mechanical and technical. However, please bear in mind that an orgasm exits the body at 28mph!

Semen contains lots of different chemicals and hormones that have a mood-elevating effect when absorbed through the vagina. This can be measured in the blood stream of a women a few hours after unprotected sex. Unfortunately as yet this test hasn't been done on semen absorbed after oral sex.

Men often will find it hard to have an orgasm if their bladder is full. So the man going to the bathroom first thing in the morning is a good idea. The feet are also linked to problems having orgasms; if a man's feet are cold his body gives out signs he needs to urinate. This also can explain why, if a man has cold feet, he will be up and down to the bathroom at night; a nice pair of warm socks or a blanket over the bottom of the bed can solve that problem.

A touchy subject for men can be the idea of the 'male P-spot' orgasm. This doesn't depend on ejaculation or even the penis; massaging the prostate with a finger or a stimulator such as an Aneros does this. The Aneros will be carefully, and with lots of lube, pushed into the man's anus. This takes lots of time and care, but can build up a trusting bond between you and your partner and produce amazing orgasms that can last up to a minute long!

Sole sensation

You have many nerve endings in your feet; they also have miniature chakra points on them. So if you masturbate with your knees open and your feet together you will find it will intensify your climax. You and your lover could also try masturbating in front of each other with both the soles of your feet touching, however, most women point their toes when the reach orgasm, so you might become on point to your lovers feet!

Foot massage is wonderful for stimulating the energy centers; try sitting facing each other but slightly off to one side with your outer leg straight so your lover can massage it while you massage their outer leg. Bend your inner leg so the foot is resting on the knee of your straight leg. I call this 'I infinity I' position or i8i. The inner legs together make the figure of 8 infinity sign. This is stimulating in two ways, the eye contact, but also the touching of such a sensitive area as the feet. If you do this naked it's also a very open view.

The energy system around the Body

A holistic view to sex is very important, you are more than a body or your thoughts or your feelings, you are a biochemical electromagnetic energy system. In fact you are a system of systems working together. All these systems are interdependent upon one another and can affect one another greatly. You are familiar with the physical body and the various systems that are contained within it, but you also have subtler bodies, which exist in the same space as the physical body but at different levels of vibration. You are more like the image of the Russian Doll made up of different levels, each level reflecting and corresponding with the levels above and below it in the overall structure. These energy bodies cannot be seen because they are composed of energy vibrating at frequencies outside of our normal range of perception. It is a higher, more refined vibration. Whenever we touch or lay next to someone there is an exchange of this energy flow. The flow is also exchanged through conversation. Although the energy cannot ordinarily be seen, it can be felt.

The etheric Body & the Aura

It is agreed by scientists that we all possess a physical aura or energy field. Infrared energy is radiated from our body as well as electrostatic and electrical ion fields, electromagnetic radiation (radio waves) and low frequency radiation of as much as one hundred kilocycles. It's amazing that we don't all come with a government health warning! However, many of us struggle to be able to put a finger on what this energy feels like. It simply feels like 'life', it feels like a warm or a cold body; when someone dies you can see that something is missing from their 'life lessbody'. Life is what is missing. The energy of this life is what is interesting. Life is made of emotion. Emotion a blur of colors all mixing into one; when we examine our feelings from those times we have been in love we find that it is made-up of touch, of joy, diluted by lots of anxiety. That anxiety could also be described as excitement.

Now we get to the bits that perhaps you have never considered before, or have only partial understanding of the subtle bodies. Your aura is part of your energy body and is a field of energy, which surrounds your physical body. This bubble of energy's job is to mark your territory and protect you from outside energies. It is like your personal force field.

In a healthy individual, the aura extends naturally about one arm's length from the body and should be bright with no holes. If we begin to feel out of balance, it may show in the aura. The aura may expand or contract. In an unhealthy or depleted aura, the aura may be dull or darker with actual holes, tears and bulges, indicating that it is not operating as it should and it will be close to the body. You literally take up less space. Using all its energy to fight infection, the aura may even contract so much that it retreats to within the physical body itself.

Not only are our thoughts and emotions on display in our body language and facial expressions, 70% of our communication is unspoken, but it is also in our aura, which can be picked up by other people. The aura is a large energy field encircling the physical body which is divided into different layers that can be seen with the physical eyes or the inner senses, and may be detected by touch. One of these is the Uric field; it is the cause of our sense of 'personal body space'. Very often we react subconsciously, saying that we have a 'gut feeling' about someone. If we feel comfortable with a person's aura we are a lot happier about allowing them into our personal space; if someone is threatening or too intense we tend to step back from them to allow us some space from their field.

The aura displays our thoughts and feelings, there is a part of us that can see or sense the aura, for example even if someone is smiling and yet you know that they are sad. We frequently use colors to describe feelings: "feeling blue", "seeing red", "in the pink", a "yellow-bellied coward" or "green with envy". The aura, on an energetic level, appears as an egg-shaped field made of millions upon millions of suspended particles of light of every color. The law of resonance shows that when physical, mental and emotional energies move in the body corresponding colored particles in the aura become activated and the aura reflects the state of the individual *as a whole energy system.*

Think of emotions as having colors. Just as it is the *wavelength* of light that determines where it will appear on the spectrum, so too different emotions have a particular energy frequency, color and sound and they are linked to specific organs and specific parts of the body. You know when you are confused about your feelings it can feel like all the colors are mixed up and any child with a paint box will tell you what you get when you mix up all the colors: a dark and dirty mess. It's the same in the aura; a confused person can look like a confusing wash of color. Removing each color layer by layer can give us back that clarity. If we are clear about what we want, then the color – and the energy signature that we transmit – is clear. This means we are giving a clear message to our lover and so be less likely to confuse a difficult day with a lack of wanting to connect sexually. It's not important to go through any aura cleansing routine; a simple intention is often enough. If you do want to do something specific try visualizing light coming from your shower when you take one, this will do the trick.

Using your life-force energy when making love

There is another form of energy that comes through us. It's hard to say if this energy is what Reiki practitioners use to aid healing, or if the spiritual healers sending loving energy heal in this way, but what I do know is energy is tangible. You can feel it, know it, be changed by it. To me it's a universal energy, like the energy of creation or life force itself. Eastern martial arts experts call this energy Chi. I have seen Chi do amazing things, set fire to paper, chop wood in half, and block a man's stomach from being stabbed. Not having done any of these things myself I can only talk about how I have felt it. I have felt it through healing and when I set about a strong intention. There is an old saying among practitioners of Eastern martial arts:

You can live for a few weeks without food. You can live for a few days without water. You can live for a few minutes without air, but you cannot live for one second without Chi.

Chi is a universal energy that permeates everything. It is also called Ki, Prana, Life-Energy or Life-Force. It is not entirely dissimilar to "The Force" described by Yoda in the movie *Star Wars*. The ancient masters who first became aware of this universal energy noticed that it is strongest around life forms and particularly strong in nature around large areas of forest, mountains and bodies of moving water. They linked it with oxygen and consequently breath, and indeed it is through the breath primarily that one learns to cultivate and manipulate this universal energy, but ultimately it is a form of energy in its own right. Not the subtlest, but certainly it is the highest-grade energy available to us on the Earth Plane. It is the life-force itself, the divine energy of creation and is part of that which sustains and moves through everything-that-is.

Thai Chi and martial arts concentrate on cultivating and manipulating chi energy. Some martial artists are capable of apparently superhuman feats using chi. Chi practitioners claim that chi can be used: to slow the aging process, move objects using the power of thought, communicate with animals and even plants, withstand pain and other amazing powers. On a more everyday level, the amount of chi you have available to you will determine your vitality; literally how much life energy you feel flowing through you. When you have life force flowing through you while making love, you pass on this wonderful energy to your partner. It's like plugging into each other's life force and sharing that energy.

Exercise: Experience Chi for yourself

This universal energy is available to us all at all times, so in order to get a real experience of this energy, to really feel it, take five minutes now to do the following exercise. Sit comfortably, and spend a moment becoming aware of your breath. Rub your hands together vigorously for a few seconds until you feel heat developing between your palms. Then hold your hands twelve inches from each other. You may begin to sense a tingling sensation in your palms and on your fingers. You can move your hands back and forth to feel the energy. This is chi. Now slightly curve your fingers as if you were holding a ball. Send through intention your love and your power into that space between your hands. Wait a time as you do this for the energy to build. Then slowly try and close your hands together. You will feel some resistance in the gap, as if you are holding a spongy rubber ball. This is your chi, your life force, and hopefully you will have just demonstrated two things to yourself; firstly that chi is real and can be felt; and secondly, that it responds to thought and intention, and can be manipulated. With this in mind it is possible, just through intention without any long classes, to use this energy when making love.

Other energy centers you can use for sex:

Root/ Kundalini chakra

Your root chakra symbolized by the color red, also known as the Kundalini, is the energy center of our sexual desire. Kundalini is the Hindu word for the sacred. The energy of the Kundalini chakra is transformative in the way that it can be a bridge between the physical body and our consciousness. This energy is like a snake coiled at the base of the spine waiting to unfold its power and potential. The awakening of this energy is called a Kundalini awakening. As this energy moves up through the chakras, it is usually sensed as an energetic force in the body, together with a strong sense of awareness of consciousness. It can be experienced as a rushing streaming up the spine, in a coiling spiral motion. When you see medical signs of the two snakes it looks how the feeling feels.

The awakening for some is a gentle process that develops as a natural consequence of many years dedicated to meditation or yoga. Others have what's known as a spiritual emergency, which is caused by an abrupt awakening; a common catalyst for this is intense physical or emotional distress. They then experience levels of awareness that they are unable to handle; they may feel highly vulnerable and oversensitive to the world around them. This causes them to become more involved with their inner processes and thoughts; they may not be able to look after themselves even in basic self-care such as washing and eating.

The process of Kundalini awakening will be different from one person to another. Some have physical symptoms, while others emotional or psychological. The new energy brings to the surface any unresolved physical or emotional issues for resolution and release. A person may experience intense involuntary movements of the body including shaking, vibrations, spasms and unusual breathing patterns, variations in sexual desire and even spontaneous orgasm. People can also experience visual phenomena, including lights, symbols, or review of past life experiences. They may report hearing voices, music, or mantras. With the opening up of intuitive abilities, a person may experience precognition, telepathy, and an awareness of auras.

Some people try to attain awaking using tantric forms of sexual activity during masturbation. It's important if you are considering an awakening of this kind to know someone you can call upon for help if it turns into an emergency. I would certainly read up on this fully before undertaking the practice of it.

Sacral chakra

The Orange Sacral chakra is the energy center of our emotions. You might recognize this from having a 'gut' instinct. This will be your Sacral chakra's reaction; I doubt your guts are doing more than digesting food! It is also where you feel it when you are concerned or worrying. You can also feel it in a good way, such as butterflies in your tummy when you are in a new relationship.

You can build a connection with this chakra by moving your hands in a circular motion around the stomach. This will bring waves of emotional safety; best done when you are lying flat on your back and even better to do this as an exchange with your partner. By rubbing your hands together you open your own energy centers of chi on the palms of your hands, you could also build the energy ball, you then place those now warm and energy-filled hands on to the Sacral chakra (abdomen) of your partner. This can send a shock of energy, which will travel straight into the orgasmic energy core. A very nice trick!

Using props to stimulate the senses and build intuition

When wanting to develop sensitive intuition it needs to be tested so you can build real confidence that you can read how a person is feeling. Your partner can be turned on and you can read that from them accurately, but how can you read if there is something that they would like you to add to what you're doing. To do this the connection needs to be deeper, but if you're focused on making the connection deeper, you can lose the focus of lovemaking – it's a delicate balance. We all have likes and dislikes; it's being able to intuitively know what someone is 'indifferent' to that's the key. You can be indifferent to a way in which your breast, buttock, neck is being held, or it can be sending shock waves of pleasure through your body. Your partner might also misread this and think it's what they are doing with the other hand, and break the magic. One way to help build the confidence to 'just know' is by using food.

Sex and food

Anything that goes into an orifice can be seen as sexual. Eating opposite each other at a restaurant or at home can be very arousing if both of you are paying attention and focusing on the other's face, mouth and their moves. Many TV advertising have used this as a way of using sex to sell a product. Haagen Dazs ice cream and Cadbury's Flake to name but two.

Feeding your partner or allowing yourself to be fed is a trust building but also a very sensual experience. If you use a blindfold your ability to really taste the food and feel the texture in your mouth as it become filled will be heightened. When one sense is denied all of the other senses become heightened including our sixth sense so you can also build your intuition. You can learn to sense if you are going to be presented with sweet or savory food; feed them and see if you can tell which food they love, which they are indifferent about and which is back in your hand! A blindfold used during sex acts much in the same way.

Food aphrodisiacs have been tested and found to have very little results in science because the placebo effectiveness was just as strong; therefore anything you set out with the intention to turn you on will probably do so. An example: Vanilla is said to increase the blood flow to the penis, that doesn't mean you have to a mouth full of ice cream when given a blow job, although if done carefully that can be fun, more a case of eating it before sex or having some vanilla oil on an oil burner in the bedroom. Either way if you intend for it to work, it will.

Daft food facts:

Testosterone is helped to release by Oatmeal.

Muira Puama makes a good herbal Viagra.

Avocados have folic acid, vitamin B6 and potassium which will lift your libido as well as your energy.

Chocolate contains phenylethylamine, which is a chemical given off in the body when we fall in love.

Open the senses

As you are a deeply sensual being playing with the normal five senses, when you remove one of them you become more aware of the sixth sense. For example if you are in an all-white room with nothing in it, how would you know what you were? When something else comes into the room, you know yourself by the contradiction to that thing. Such as if a Baby came into the room, you would know your age, or if a Cat came into the room you would know the cat is soft and you are not.

Experiment with introducing elements (such as the ones described below) into your sexual moments and remove them on other occasions as your senses will get used to them, seek them out and through seeking we become more open; and the sixth sense is found.

Essential oils and scents

Lavender helps a man keep an erection; maybe those old ladies that put packets of it in the knickers draw knew what they were doing after all! *Jasmine, ylang-ylang, rose, sandalwood* and *juniper* are said to bring about sexual desire. You can also get a patch called *Scentuelle* that is impregnated with scents to give you sexual feelings. This is designed for women, to be worn during the day and keep smelling it to trigger sexual lust.

Making love to music

Many people discover this by playing music when they

masturbate so the rest of the household won't hear any noise that comes out of the bedroom. Music can be very sexy and it doesn't have to be Barry White blasting out of your speakers. Choose your tunes carefully; in these days of itunes and iPods, it makes making a compilation CD or a section on your iPod for lovemaking simple. Think about what kind of mood you want to set. Soft and relaxing for long slow sex, strong beats for faster more dynamic lovemaking. You could try matching thrusts with the beat. You can also bring on your orgasm by listening to the build in the music that might help you and your lover to be able to cum at the same time.

Sex during menstruation

Both women and men can find having sex at this time a little messy and off-putting. It depends largely on the person. Some men can also really love it and have no problem giving oral stimulation to their partner at this time of the month. I have named this the VCC or Vampire clit club! Mainly due to an erotic description of this in one of the Anne Rice Vampire Chronicles.

At this time of the month a woman's vagina is highly sensitive. There is extra blood in the lining of the walls meaning during slow penetrative sex she can feel every small groove of ridge in her man's erect penis. The blood flow of the period isn't as much during sex, although it may look like it is as it is mixed with the female arousal lubrication. Orgasm can also help with stomach cramps, for some even making the period pains go away during sex. For many women it can feel like an act of real love. It gives the message, "I love and except you completely as a woman." A very powerful energy-giving feeling.

Back in history woman were seen as unclean when they menstruated and were not to be touched. My theory on all of this is to do with religious viewpoints of the time. Some organized religions wanted people to wait until they were married before having sex. Due to the lack of contraception there was an obvious result of sex before marriage but it was thought to be less likely for a woman to become pregnant during menstruation (although many women do) so it was used as a form of contraception. This would make it possible to 'sin' with someone you weren't married too and not have to pay the consequence. However, by making sure strange rules were abided to such as women not being allowed to wash their hair and making everyone believe that they have 'the curse', it tied up that loophole.

Visual stimulation and Cybersex

We are in a world where isolation is becoming more common than personal face-to-face communication. However, now more than at any other time people have a mass of information open to them. The Internet has made so many things accessible in the home that otherwise would only be available in some of the seedier parts of town. I remember going to see a peep show when I lived in Australia. You put a dollar in the slot, a window opened and a girl played with her vibrator as she lay across the floor. Only if she was caught unaware she read a book in the corner of the room. My boyfriend and I would wait a few minutes before putting in the dollar, to see if we could catch which book she was reading! Now this kind of thing is available at home. A woman might never consider her boyfriend's fantasy of a threesome; yet a girl online with a webcam and you and your partner giving instructions on what you want her to do for the credit card payment would be different. Women are more likely to allow worrying about getting a computer virus to get in the way of being turned on over the Internet. You can also buy a USB adapter for your computer which vibrates; this means you can hold it between your legs while chatting online.

Chatting online to other couples or even on your own and taking part in cybersex can be great fun. It's safe if you don't give away any personal information and it's anonymous. An older woman can be messaging a much younger man and having fantastic cybersex without worrying about stretch marks and cellulite. It's the sexy and exciting things we crave without any of the hang-ups. It also can be very loving because there is nothing to worry about; you can say what you like and make very deep connections with someone it is likely you would never meet. Often it's a good idea not to meet them. Anyone who has seen the scene in the film version of Patrick Marber's 'Closer', with Jude Law and Natalie Portman, can remember the scene when Dan (*Jude Law*), who is pretending to be a woman called Anna, has great cybersex with Larry (*Clive Owen*) who is a doctor. Dan asks Larry to meet and go to a hotel, which Larry does only to find he is the victim of a writer with too much time on his hands.

I wouldn't endorse moving from meeting in a cybersex virtual bedroom to a real one unless you really feel you must, and if so, splash out on a hotel where you can leave and have lots of people in the rooms around you if you need to get out of a situation.

Porn is available to most people's taste, although intuitive people often dislike porn. This can be because being intuitive you can read and see when someone isn't comfortable. If you tune in to their emotions and feelings in that moment and see what is really happening and it is not a wholly enjoyable experience for them, it will put you off entirely. Finding really good video and photographic porn that any women would be into can also be difficult, as women generally don't respond to this type of porn.

Absence makes the heart grow fonder

The Internet can be used as a great way of keeping sexual contact when you are not around each other. In the first flush of new romance we have a bond strengthened by chemicals in the brain. Hormones and neurochemicals race round the brain caused by the touch, taste and smell of your partner. Just hugging realizes oxytocin into the brain, which makes us feel the emotion of trust.

These chemicals match those created by many drugs such as Ecstasy or cocaine. Some people can actually become addicted to love; in this state your partner's well-being can become more important than your own.

When you become separated from your partner, for example, your partner going away on business for a week can bring about intense feelings of loss and fear. If that partner then forgets to call when they say they will, the reaction can be the same craving as a drug addict would go through. Take a moment to just think about how many songs have been written about this state of feeling; describing driving all night to get next to you, or bleeding love. It's painfully ecstatic and can define the relationship into a much deeper state when you finally are back together.

What if the relationship ends at this point?

I hate to bring it up, but sometimes this point the relationship ends. Say for example a holiday romance, someone going away to university. The partner is already in a relationship and can't commit or they meet someone else or simply don't want to be with you, the hurt can be profoundly devastating. A sense of closure of these feelings needs to happen before you may feel you can move on. Even if the person turned out to be a lying toerag, the chemical addiction to them can override the logical mind. It can be looked at like any addiction. We know cigarettes, heroin, and alcohol are bad, but it doesn't mean you can just change your mind and quit; it's not always that easy.

It takes the act of being kind to you. Try hard not to analyze the person's choices; the chances are they won't have logic to them anyway, our emotions often don't. Focus the mind on the other positive events and stay reasonably busy. Don't allow your mind to stay focused on the ex-partner. Replace thoughts of them as often as possible with other thoughts. If you feel suicidal or a little crazy with the emotions seek help. You might feel stupid but you are the victim of hormonal overload. Friends often tell people to 'get over it' or 'move on'; you might be kind not to remind them of this when it happens to them, because undoubtedly, unless they are very lucky (or unlucky), it happens to everyone.

If only someone had told Romeo and Juliet that it would pass!

The shift from being 'In love' to being loving

We do eventually shift from 'I can't be without you' to 'I'm out tonight, see you tomorrow'. For some the loss of the intensity can feel alarming. The relationship can feel flat and you might question, "Is this really the 'one' after all?" The brain chemicals calm down, and they would need to; looking after children, looking after the home and going to work with that intense emotion would be hard work.

The relationship is now moving into a very important stage, sex can grow and become stronger or it can just tick along. It just depends how you would like your consciousness to grow. Read on...

Part Three: Conscious Love

As we grow with our relationship partner we become a full expression of ourselves. Through intuition we help guide our partner through life's obstacles. We also use intuition as a personal guidance system to help ourselves become the best that we can be; both in the relationship and life's journey itself.

You don't have to get married to know that you are with your life partner, something just clicks. The way you know is that you can't conceive of your life without them.

Most people have an expectation of life often based from what we hear in the media; statistics based on an average. Society seems to believe that everyone gets married, has two kids, holds down a job, then gets divorced, becomes a single mother with father fighting for visitation rights or quits and runs off with the younger office sectary. We don't often hear positive reports about anything in life and this goes for long-term relationships too. However, I doubt that you reading this or I writing it would endorse the idea of an 'ordinary' life. Therefore nothing negative you have ever heard about relationships need apply to you! In fact your relationship is breaking new ground, love and connection never experienced before. Now we have set out that intention, from this point the style of how you want to live your life together is up to you. You don't have to conform to the socially acceptable relationship. You have the power as a couple to make up the rules between the two of you as you go along though life. You are more likely to stick to plans, ideas and rules if they have come from your own choice and have the added advantage of being flexible. It's important to check in with your partner's growth and change in thought patterns. Often we decide on something, and change our mind when we have new evidence. Couples can often think they know everything there is to know about their partner. For example, has your favorite flavor of ice cream changed throughout the years? I would expect so; therefore it makes sense that our preferred sexual position or way of being held and kissed will also change too. Our ideas of being monogamous many also change; however, we often fear broaching these questions, seen to be dangerous ground and the start of the end of the relationship. Just bringing up the subject could be the start of the divorce papers.

I admire people who can have the absolute certain knowledge that they have met the person they want to marry and that no matter what happens in the future they 100% believe they will stick to those marriage vows, through sickness and in health, for better or for worse. Still sometimes there maybe someone else you desperately want to sleep with, get to know or become fascinated by. This often crops up just at the point where your current partnership is having a crisis. Also ask any person on the eve of their wedding and you might find that pre-wedding nerves are having a strong impact on their evening. Often there is a feeling of bereavement even after marrying the person of your dreams. This loss is for who we were in our single life. This can happen after marriage, moving in with a person or even sometime later. A bit of us dies and a new us needs to grow. We are often happy to acknowledge this at the end of a relationship but not during. Whenever our circumstance changes even for the better, we can have a sense of loss. It can be wise to discuss this carefully with your partner, help each other through your personal changes, the chances are you're not alone in this and your partner might just be wondering what's wrong.

We never know what is going to happen in our future. We also don't know who we will be in our future depending on what life changing events mold us into a new way of thinking and being. For me if I was getting married, my vows might be along the lines of, "I intend to spend the rest of my life with you. I can't promise but with every ounce of my power I will do everything to make this work." I would also ask that everyone one attending the wedding become tools to help us both stick to our powerful intention. Meaning when I am having a rough time and having a moan to a friend about something my partner has done, that my friend doesn't indulge me in the traditional friendship, "He didn't!...The bastard," and that they slap me into shape by reminding me of the love that still burns deep inside and that our ego for each other is getting out of alignment with our love. As yet I haven't made this intention to anyone. The moment I do, it will be with my body, mind and spirit, or I won't do it at all and spend the rest of my life having light fascinating relationships that take me to a limited but wondrous growth. The long haul relationship is the one of ultimate personal growth. I say ultimate personal growth because you will be tested, stretched, frustrated, deeply and profoundly connected to someone that knows you inside out. Achieving and keeping this connection is the journey that leads to this growth.

Keeping sexual attraction, lust and even lovemaking with one person offers a new challenge. It's true that the more you are with someone and have a deeper connection with them or 'soul mate', you begin to think the same, have the same friends, likes and dislikes but the more you lose the polarity of sexual desire. It is the difference between us that makes us sexually desire our partner. Blending to become one and the same person makes us: best friends, brothers and sisters, but sadly not lovers. What separates us is more sexually attractive than the soulmate connection. When we see our partners as individuals, people in their own right outside of our relationship with them, we find them more attractive. It is difficult to feel sexy about one half of ourselves and yet that is what we call our partner, 'our other half'!

It is a controversial point as most people are looking for someone who will complete them, but in fact what works for a long-term sexual relationship is someone who compliments rather than completes. The yin and yang symbol is a great representation of this:

The black and the white interlocks, both have a little bit of each, but both are totally different: male and female polarity. We need to have a difference to be able to have sexual attraction. So even as soulmates you need to see each other as being separate from yourself to make the connection of coming together sexually. Having a life outside of each other's lives together and being able to talk about that and share it is a deeper bond. You might feel uncomfortable about your partner having friends whom you have never met or going to events you are not invited too, but all of this helps to build the separateness in your togetherness. The space that shows you to be separate and the coming together which reminds you that you chose each other.

Challenge

One of the biggest challenges in a long-term relationship is not allowing the comfort of your togetherness to turn into boredom. Boredom in the bedroom is highly likely as we get so used to our partners moves, and so body fantasies of other partners and scenarios feel more exiting. This isn't a case of wanting our cake and eating it too; it's the human need to be stretched and grow. With our partner we know what they want and what turns them on, from this point we need to stretch our comfort zone and boundaries with our partner to keep that sexual progression. We enjoy a first time kiss, first time sex or a risk that gives extra sexual bite of anxiety and fear. With our long-time lover we don't have this, so we need to create it. This is again where your intuition can play a part. Allowing you to feel where your partner's limit is and push them very gently into unknown zones of pleasure they may not have expected. It is also about real honest communication. Often we don't express some of our darker fantasies for fear of upsetting our partner or making ourselves look like a pervert, but now you're in this committed relationship and for the salvation of your sex life you can start to open the eyes wide and become honest about the things you have thought about doing in the past. Baring your soul to this 'darker side' of your sexual fantasy involves danger and anxiety, which are the emotions we feel though first time sex. Adding an exciting dynamic to your life with each other, allowing you to feel truly accepted, deepens the relationship and keeps the sex life interesting.

We often focus on what we don't want in our life rather than focusing on what we do. Also we often want to use our will to change the direction and actions of our partner; we of course can't change anyone else but ourselves but this is enough. If you find yourself pulling focus on the negative aspects of your sex life or relationship try a visualization exercise.

Exercise: Perfection visualization

Close your eyes and view the relationship in six months time exactly the way that you want it. Bring in whatever you feel is missing; see it play out on the big cinema screen that is your imagination. Now move backwards in time watching all of the events that unfold from this point in time to that perfect point in the future. What is the difference in the way you are acting now to the way you are acting then? Don't focus on what your lover needs to do differently, just you. Now try acting as if you have this in your relationship now. This may change the way your partner is also acting; it can also change your perception of the situation. By focusing on what we have that is positive and focusing on the positive change, we don't bring into the relationship more of what we don't want, we bring in more of what we do!

The vibrational spectrum of woman

The question of faithfulness is one that will plague many relationships. It is the cause of fear and anxiety for both men and women. Deception can lead to the break-up of the family unit. Possibly causing you to become a single parent or loosing regular access to your children and the trust is hard to rebuild. However, a deeper understanding of your drives, both life focus and sex drives, can lead to a greater balance and make you less likely to look for another person outside the committed partnership.

There is a stereotypical belief that men are ruled by their penis. This view is untrue and insulting. Men have a far greater desire of women; this is to embrace the whole feminine spectrum of vibration. Men can become confused by this spectrum of feminine energy; they can become distracted by it unless they understand fully what it is and how it can affect them.

For example a woman who loves her shoes and has lots of them might one day feel like she needs brown leather or black patent, a high heel or a pump. The choice of these many shoes gives her the feeling of wholeness. The shoes allow her to feel all of the different kinds of woman that are within her. Her shoe changes her walk and her feminine dynamic, the energy changes in her from the feet up. Having this choice is important and one most women may relate to but this can be found in many things other than shoes; a choice of perfume or coffee and cake, having lots of knick-knacks around the home or one very choice beautiful object. These things allow us to feel whole and full as a person, these are in a sense: soul nutrients. Men are attracted to women in a similar way to this. Men look for women in the infinite expressions of feminine energy. Men look for that feeling of fullness in themselves: through women.

In everyday life a man can go from one state of attraction from a woman to another. He might see a lady walk by with a summer dress on, get a glimpse of her legs as the summer sun turns the dress into being see-through. He might like the girl who pushes past him on the bus and gives him a look of disdain. It might be the lady in the office in a power suit and heels. Women have so many ways they show the female vibration: The cool icy woman, the demure woman, powerful businesswoman. Men love the full spectrum of feminine energy. The Spice Girls really hit female sexual archetypes on a winning note: Sporty Spice (hot, sweaty and fit), Baby Spice (take care of and dominate this sweet girl), Scary Spice (be dominated), Ginger Spice (kind of dirty and smutty) and Posh Spice (thinks she's too good for you, but breaks under seduction). Just part of the whole spectrum of women. Their music would never have really mattered with such a winning combination vibration.

New sex with a woman from a different vibration is exciting to men. Many men would sacrifice their marriage, children and home to have a taste of this variation. We have seen this in men of great political power that have been on the edge of losing everything and even lied to their country just to experience this spectrum of vibration. But before all women bury their woe into a new pair of Birkenstock and give up on men completely, as the song goes 'I'm EVERY woman, it's All in me!' Every variation of the feminine rainbow spectrum is in each woman. The more a woman can stay in her inspired self the more she allows herself to be creative with her expression of femininity. One evening she goes out in a powerful high heel, the next in a sporty trainer. Our clothes also give us our attitude in our costume of expression. To be truly attractive to men, your body doesn't matter, your attitude and vibration does. We have all wondered why a great-looking guy is with less attractive women. It is the vibration we send out, not what we look like, that makes the difference. A woman can play all sounds to keep her man interested, all vibrations of the sexual polarity between male and female.

Men maybe attracted by a full spectrum of women, but it doesn't mean he wants to sleep with them. Commitment is different to attraction. He wants to merge with this feminine vibration. This is natural and innocent. A man can breathe in the vibration of these women. He may feel he wants to flirt, having an innocent kind of verbal sex. As the feminine energy is life force energy you can find that energy through nature, a walk in the woods, a swim in the ocean. Anything that involves restriction that breaks through into release can be enough to curb the cravings. The male vibration needs something to resist him, the seduction leading to sex and finally the release of the orgasm. For many men they can't think of anything else until they have this release. The tension must come before. Any form of tension will do; this is why men tend to love football, the tension before the release of the goal. Even wars come about through this tension before the freedom of or from religious expression or more land.

The build-up of this sexual energy, the need for release can be channeled into personal inspiration. In fact it can have nothing to do with sex at all. We can take being turned on by someone outside of the relationship and the energy of desperately wanting to have sex with them and use that energy as inspiration for other projects. Artists and writers may have a muse. This person may make them feel alive and young, which can be an inspiration for our greatest gift we have to give the world. Poets often say they write much better when there is a conflict at heart. This doesn't mean going out of your way to string along someone sexually, but understanding that sexual energy is not lost just because it's not used for sex. You can take that energy into the bedroom with your partner but that isn't always possible. Desire is a form of inspiration; you can use sexual desire and the energy of that to follow your life's purpose with the same invigoration as the lust of an untapped attraction.

Following your life's purpose
Both as men and woman we have a purpose something we are really good at, our gift to the world, our talent. Ask the question, "What is the greatest gift you want to give the world?" Our

purpose shows us the gift we want to give; this becomes our personal inspiration for everything we do. Our purpose isn't something we think, it is something we feel, and from that feeling comes all of our actions. It is the unchangeable part of us. The relationship we are in can be a representation of that gift. Your partnership can serve that purpose or it can work out of alignment with it.

For finding this purpose, take time away from all distractions. This could be 30 minutes every day or a week or a month of solitude. In this time stop doing and start feeling. Find the source of every thought that comes to your mind. Sit in silent meditation allowing thoughts to come and go, each time looking for the source of these thoughts, until a bubble of emotion and idea starts to rise. This bubble is a knowing. Inside this knowing comes the source of why you decided to be born. To answer the question, "What do I need to give to the world so I can live everyday with purpose?" There is no single way of life that suits everyone but when you know your purpose you can decide if fidelity fits that purpose or if an open relationship fits better.

Then take time for the next question, "What is the greatest gift you want to give this partnership?" "Who is the best of You?" Over time relationships loose the sexual polarity of the masculine and feminine as we become in a partnership. That partnership might become being about taking care of the children or the home. This may cause the sex in the relationship to almost disappear. Expecting to keep working together as a team with the responsibilities of life and keep the sexual polarity is a lot to ask. Think about what is the single most important reason for you two to be together, then organize your sex around that; if it's your children, sex comes second to your children's needs. What keeps you both together as a partnership is the important thing; the partnership often needs a purpose in order to help it weather time. Don't put you or your partner under pressure by expecting that you can do everything all at once.

Balance is what is needed and putting forward what is the most important thing in that moment, so as not to become overwhelmed by the needs of life and of the relationship. If you work together well in the day, the chances are you'll feel the desire at night but the goal in the partnership keeps the link together if sex has to take a very far back seat. If you both feel that you are too merged as a couple you need to find space to bring back the polarity. Role-play can be a good way of redefining your separate energies even if it means dressing up as the subservient maid or stable boy. Just taking time to connect through the masculine and feminine energy will bring back a sense of sexual polarity. There is a section in this book on kinks, refer to this if you need something to keep the masculine and feminine energy balance. This is what is meant by sexual spark, the bigger spark is caused by the bigger polarity.

Stay fully present
Intuitive knowing and paying attention to subtle signals is no substitute for really listening to our partners; really hearing someone is not an easy thing. It demands real concentration, it can be exhausting but on the whole one of the most rewarding gifts we can give. Our own experience of being listened to in our childhood helps to mold our feelings of self-worth. As a teenager I watched the film *The Breakfast Club*, it's a film about a group of American teenagers held in a school detention on a Saturday. They span the range of stereotypes of the time but each character reveals problems at home, some of the problems involve even physical harm. Until the most messed up of the characters revels her problems are 'real bad' as her parents ignore her; throughout the film she will try anything to get attention.

When we don't feel fully heard we will often resort to acts outside of our character to get the attention we are looking for; a woman may smash her partner's CD collection, rip up his clothes or even sleep with his best friend to get attention. Men are less likely to need to be heard. Men will often want to work things out for themselves before entering into discussion but because of this when he does enter into the subject realm of what he has been thinking about, he needs to be really heard.

To really listen to what someone is saying we need to think about what is being said and understand what's being excluded. This is a form of intuitive listening where you are not only hearing the words but the silence and the pauses in-between. You can ask questions and maybe even repeat the odd word of what you are hearing. In normal conversation we are often waiting for our cue to reply and share a similar story. As soon as we know what we want to say we often stop listening and wait for our moment; the conversation flow or a subject has sometimes moved on and we stop the rhythm by wanting to make our point, however, we wouldn't know as we've stopped listening. In many families, including my own, when we get together five conversations take place at once. I might be asked a question and in the middle of replying, my mother will make a comment into a conversation that's going on behind her. Most of us have the ability to be aware of everything else going on around us at the same time as being in a conversation with someone; this isn't listening, but a fantastic skill if you want to be a military spy! Listening is an emotional connection, it involves empathy and connection. For the majority of women this is the first line of foreplay; we find it such an attractive quality in a person, even if they are just a friend, listeners are the kind of people you long to keep in your life.

Tips for being a great listener:

- Engage your facial expression. Nod, look interested and keep eyes connected. Smile encouragingly.
- Make the odd 'uh-huh' sounds.
- Move your body slightly forward so you are leaning towards the person.

- Try not to talk about yourself in return until you have fully covered your partner talking about themselves.
- Pay attention to anything your partner is asking you to do and recap to make sure you understood them correctly.

You might also like to try five minutes of silently just looking into each other's eyes before you start talking. Making a connection on a soul to soul level means you are more likely to feel your partner on a deeper level and less likely to go for the jugular when you do talk about the difficult things that you need to say. If your mind starts to wander, when you notice it just bring it back to that place of focus again.

The male head voice

A man may have two voices in his head. One voice tells him of his desire to deepen his relationship and the other will be talking him into the opportunity of new sex with a women who perhaps has a different female vibration to his current relationship situation. Knowing his deepest purpose will allow him to focus this split voice into hearing the voice of his highest intention. But only by knowing his purpose is he able to know himself and the origins of the source of this voice. Fidelity doesn't suit all people but because most people get hurt when someone is unfaithful we think of it as bad. To be unfaithful is to lose the faith of your partner; if you can be open about who you are in your highest purpose then your partner maybe comfortable with you taking other lovers under the right circumstances. Polygamous relationships can work, what is unfaithful is to lie about who we are. Of course who we are in terms of the personality will change throughout time but our purpose will stay the same. We can be deeply in love with someone's spirit and put up with examples of their ego self.

When it comes to a monogamous relationship the man must first realize his higher-self's purpose and bring about his greatest gift to the world. Then his real focus, his need to exist, will be greater than his desire for other women. Men will either realize their greatest gift or be tempted to be unfaithful, or even worse be uninspired by the relationship he has committed to, making him closed and unadventurous. When a man knows who he is he will be comfortable in knowing his own desires and more than happy to take his partner along for the ride!

Every woman who understands the deeper meaning wants her partner to be able to give this gift to the world, not because of her, but with or without her. His strength in purpose means he is strong with or without her. She can smell the weakness of a man who can't go on to fulfill himself without her feminine energy. She wants him to focus his gift into the world so she can admire and stand by him, knowing his strength comes from a pure source with no dependence on her.

You are not your thoughts but the thinker of your thoughts

As human beings we are constantly under the influence of our thoughts. People may study meditation to be able to quiet the voice in their head that chatters away all day long, sometimes even disrupting our sleep by going over and over the same event. Our thoughts may also become negative in the way we feel about ourselves: Eric Berne said that we can break this ego state into three head voices he called them the 'Parent, Adult and Child'. Even these three voices can be broken down between the positive outlook and the negative. A negative Parent might say 'I can't believe you didn't get up early to get your work done, now you're in trouble' A positive Parent would say 'You needed that sleep, I trust you to get the work done in record time now you have rested.' Your negative Adult could say 'People are going to think you're lazy.' Your positive Adult voice would say 'I don't care what people think, I know the truth'. Your negative Child voice may say 'It's not fair! I want to stay in bed!' you're positive

Child will say 'lets get up and play the game of life'. However, whichever voice rules your mind, you still have a choice. The real You is not your thoughts, those random messages we send out, but instead the real You is the thinker of those thoughts. You can put your Thinker in control at any time; your Thinker can stop the random thoughts and think again, putting in the replacement positive parent adult or child. It takes mindfulness at first but over a period of time the negative voice will get squished out.

A woman may want to verbally express her thoughts as she has them, so as her desires develop what she is asking for changes, this can confuse the man about what she really wants; it can come across that the mind change is a lie but thoughts are like the weather they are ever changing. If we believe that we are these thoughts then we can become confused about who we really are. When the Masculine and Feminine energy communicate the masculine will try and resolve thoughts into a single resolution, but when the feminine is talking that conversation for them is just about connecting with her partner gaining their attention and nothing more than that. Therefore not wanting the conversation to resolve as she is feeling satisfied with the attention; the resolution of the conversation would take away the connection she is enjoying.

Sometimes listening to someone's day can feel boring but if you stay connected to your higher-self the experience lends itself to a deeper purpose of building the connection between you. You can dance with a changing mind and be inspired by it but don't let go of the true essence of you, remember you are thinker of your thoughts.

How do you feel?

The only constant is change; our thoughts change, our emotions change, but we believe we should be able to love someone all of the time. It is impossible to love someone all the time on an ego level, but in the level of your deepest connection you can.

If your partner says something out of alignment with your thoughts you might say, "I love you so much that I have to let you know I disagree with you." The more new age view is to look at yourself and your own issues as to why you disagree with your partner. The thing to be certain of is that not expressing the disagreement and internalizing it doesn't serve the relationship. You can still come from a place of love and not accusation but be expressive; this will help to deepen the relationship. There is nothing spiritual about holding your silence, speaking your truth in love is profound.

We often ask our partner, "How they are feeling?" because as we have discussed our emotions change. We also ask this question so we can feel safe in the relationship; but in doing we open ourselves up to being lied to. Not necessarily on a large scale but by misrepresentation: for example they might be happy, but the mere fact they've been asked a question may make them feel annoyed, so the reply would be happy/annoyed. Questions like this are lazy and can throw someone off their flow. It's easy to learn to tune into your partner, and therefore deepen the partnership; simply look into the person's eyes and tune into them by taking their hand. To read our partner's emotions we have to open up, this allows our partner to also read us which builds a wonderful open connection.

Too stressed for sex

Life can feel like it's beyond our control: that things happen to us and that all we can do is cope with them on a day-to-day basis. Our sleep can be interrupted by thoughts of things we fear happening and things we have to get done the following day. It is hard in a world where all we seem to do is rush to be in a calm position where we would enjoy sex with our partner, however, imagine how stressful your life would be if you were single! When our sex life dies but we are still at a point in our life when we feel the need for physical connection, it's only a matter of time before the relationship will end. Which is really sad; when we talk about our relationship once it has ended we don't often say, "I really miss the sex." It's usually the small things and the emotional connection we miss, but sex can be an important way of enhancing the relationship and reaffirming those connections that are passed over. A stressful life can kill a sex drive, but it doesn't have to. It's about making time to be able to make the space to have sex, making sex a priority. Even if this becomes an appointment in your diary it's not a bad thing. Most of us think that sex has to be spontaneous and that booking an appointment with your lover might feel contrived. It is better to make that appointment than to miss out on having sex in your relationship. If, when the appointment comes around, you're not in the mood it only takes a bit of stimulation to set the right mood for you to get turned on.

Here are some tips on how to do that:

Turning your mind off and your body on

- When you are making love the last thing you want is to be thinking about your tax return. For a woman to become sexually turned on the mind has to be turned off! Any thought can switch the mind back on again and therefore block the pathway to an orgasm for a woman. S o m e women find it hard to switch off. Often thoughts before making love could be that of judgments about our partner. Anything they have done within the last week that has been annoying can be brought into her mind at that moment and stop her wanting to have sex. She   might be fine when masturbating alone but with them even thoughts about what they are thinking or feeling can block her own ability to feel.
- Taking up meditation would go some way to help with this problem as this is a process of learning to quiet the mind. For those with a young family it is especially difficult but

if someone else is looking after them while you have a bath or if they're having a nap take 5 minutes for this.

- Allow your mind to think in sexual pictures. Any fantasy you have to play that out in your mind.
- Remember sex can help you sleep and be a great way of preventing a build-up of stress.

Don't rush

- When you feel like you don't have time for sex you might be tempted just to give your lover what they want, excluding yourself to save a bit of time. It doesn't take long to allow yourself pleasure so just go with the flow and enjoy. You will feel far less stressed and uptight after an orgasm and build less resentment towards your partner.
- Arousal often comes after kissing, touching and other sexual acts have started but we can feel that we must feel sexy before we enter into having sex. With a busy mind, often starting the act of sex puts us into the right frame of arousal. If it doesn't then some intimate time with our partner is great for building a connection which may lead to sex the next time.

Massage

- Starting sex with a good massage is a great way to focus on the body and relax it.
- It can take months to build-up the knots in the muscles and only minutes to start to break them down and feel better. Use an oil you really like the smell of; the shop **Coco De Mer** has some wonderfully sensual sex equipment and amazing scented oils.

Music

- Playing soft music slows down the mind and will make you feel like you have the time to take it easy.

- The music can help to turn off the internal chatter.

High sex drive vs. low sex drive

Let's not lay all the need to change behavior patterns at the foot of the bed of the person with the least sex drive. It is often seen that if you don't want sex then you are the one with the problem. A person with a high sex drive can put tremendous pressure on their partner for sex, which can be offputting in itself.

Here are some tips to help you both come into alignment:

Calming down a higher sex drive:

- Are you looking for sex or a feeling of comfort and connection? Know yourself and be clear about your intentions.
- Masturbate more. Make an agreement with your partner for a bit of alone bed time or ask your partner to hold you while you masturbate. You have every right to calm your pressure down with a good orgasm.
- Accept that your partner's low libido could be caused by your lack of skills in the bedroom or a signal of problems within the relationship. Make time to talk and be open to what you may hear. You might not like it, but it might save what is working. It's very difficult to tell someone that sex once worked but now it's boring, or less attractive, but it's far better to know and fix it than lose the relationship.
- Be willing to put some seduction work in, find out what they want and be open to change. If your partner is stressed, maybe go away for the weekend. Take tips from fantasies they may have told you about and surprise them. For example if they have always wanted to be Guinevere being seduced by Lancelot behind King Arthur's round table you might like to take her to a castle and talk seductively or find one you can stay in with a big four-poster bed.

- Take up sport and wear yourself out at the gym.

Bringing up a lower sex drive:

- Look at your levels of stress and see what you can do to make time or bring them down.
- Have a bath before bedtime so you are feeling really relaxed.
- Make time to read sexual and sensual books instead of other books you normally read.
- Flirt with people outside the relationship, preferably strangers so they don't think you're leading them on by doing so. Feeling attractive always makes the libido higher.
- Make time for you away from other people and take time to enjoy your own body.

The art of seduction

The more spiritual we become the more we look at seduction as a form of power play that we don't want to take part in. We want to be able to be honest, and not coax a person into bed. Seduction seems like a lie; playing a game to make ourselves become something more attractive and so be something we are not. However, there is something deeply wonderful about being seduced; it is the stuff of great films. It also is a great compliment and self-esteem boost that we can give another person.

Seduction is something we do every day without even thinking about it. We win over our friends, family and work colleagues. Life has to be all about seduction just to get on in the world we live. When we think of seduction it seems to be reserved for new sexual encounters; if you don't seduce a person you have just met, you can move on to someone new; but it is never more important than when it is in a long-term relationship.

Instigating sex in a long-term relationship can be really hard. In some cases it can be as difficult as instigating sex for the first time with a new partner. One or both of you will have rejected sex with one another at some point due to being tired, stressed or annoyed with your partner. So there is still a memory of that rejection.

If you both haven't had sex in a long time, you might even wonder if your partner still finds you sexually attractive. You might be so scared of the answer you just don't want to find out. Feelings like that could spell the end of the relationship.

Often the seduction becomes masked in phrases such as "I'm going to have an early night" or "I'm off to bed", which can be misunderstood. It's wonderful to make someone feel wanted, even if we risk being knocked back; it opens a discussion and brings sex into the relationship equation. Using wording like: "I really want you tonight", "You turn me on, shall I see you in the bedroom?", even down to fun things like, "Fancy a shag, Sexy?!" let's your partner know you want them and using sexual wording is a great turn on.

It becomes difficult for couples when a real sexual energy block occurs. The person rejecting feels guilt and the person being rejected feels confusion and pain. We can be intuitive as to why these things are happening. However, the fear of seeing something we don't want to can block our intuition into the whole situation. Frustration and anger can also block us from intuitively seeing the truth. A sex block can often be the sign of something else emotional going on. In these more difficult situations, do see a sex therapist. It can be hard to talk about these things but is easier when you know it's for the sake of not losing someone you love due to lack of sex.

Sex long term

It's so sad that we often take for granted the idea that when two people are in a long-term relationship the sex will become less or even die out completely.

Our life can become a long 'to do list'. With work responsibilities, children and trying to make time for ourselves. All too often your partner will become at the end of the 'to do' list. When we use the word partner, we think of a person who is in our life to help with this list of life things we have to get done. The problem of raising children is halved and the household tasks shared. What it should really feel like, having someone in your life, is a sense of both of you working together as a team. This can cause your expectations not to be met; if you have been the one to clean the bathroom every time for months it can build anger and resentment. It's very hard for a woman to want to make love when she is angry. The longer you are in a relationship the need for make-up sex lessens as we tend to put up with more and not raise our voice when we are angry about a situation. So the resentment stays, this leads to lack of sex as we don't reach the point of release that a confrontation and make-up sex can bring in the early days. The idea of make-up sex loses the appeal for women also because they like to feel a connection to their partner and if the two have been in a situation of conflict then that connection won't feel solid. Make-up sex is generally much easier and passionate for a man; conflict can make the blood flow. In fact if a woman says to a man, "We need to talk," the blood will flow to the muscles making it uncomfortable physically for him to sit and have this conversation. A women needs eye contact to try and read what he isn't saying, a man needs to walk around and help move some of this blood now rushing into his leg muscles.

Relationships would suffer fewer arguments if the connection between the two were clearer and stronger. Make your partner part of your 'to do' list and therefore make essential time for each other. If you are a morning person, set the alarm twenty minutes before you need to get up. Twenty minutes will make little difference to how tired you feel during the day, or set aside twenty minutes at any point in the day to be fully present with your partner.

Often people become scared if they believe that you will find something or someone that you love more than them. This doesn't mean an affair, but any person that you prefer to spend time with other than them. This can mean that your partner will stand in the way of some of your friendships as they fight off any threat to getting your 100% attention. This is generally more true of women than men but by giving your partner full attention at some point in the day, it will lessen the risk of becoming a problem. There is a balance between living your life's greatest gift and having your partner love you more for it, and your partner feeling they are going to lose you to something bigger than they are in your life. This of course comes down to their personal self-esteem but making time can help alleviate the feelings of insecurity.

Sex doesn't always have to be amazing; it can just be about touching and holding each other, but do try and give time for amazing sex too. Amazing mind blowing sex doesn't often start in the bedroom. It starts by going out for a drink, being in the cinema holding hands. It starts by a simple sexual intention, but it is conducted with the intention of making your partner feel loved, valued and just great about themselves.

What is Love anyway?

It is our deepest longing not to be alone. Even if we don't choose a life partner we want our lives to be filled with Love, every different kind of love available;

- Romantic love where we are made to feel special and sacred to another person;
- Physical love where our body is desired and wanted to be held, touched, to enter and be entered into.

We long to be linked to another person by their approval, validation, forgiveness, respect, devotion, closeness, compassion, kindness, support. We long to feel nurtured, and to be the one and only to give and nurture in return. We believe this will give us a life full of peace, joy and happiness. We only need to find the 'one' right person. We learn this deep from childhood where we get attention and appreciation when we do the 'right' thing and please our parents or teachers. Often when we are growing up love is withheld when we are naughty and given if we have been good. We learn that Love has boundaries that must not be crossed if it is to stay alive. Abandonment surely means death as we know we cannot survive without each other. So we learn how to hold others to ransom to the production or lack of production of love.

By thinking like this we limit true Love. Loving is an infinite energy; it is in fact the creative energy that starts off everything. Love is the only energy that was in the beginning. Love is the energy that broke into millions of peaces at the moment of the big bang. Everything that you see in the world has been made by it. Even every man-made thing has been built through Love. We build homes for our loved ones, cars, boats trains, and our passion for travel. Even bombs were built through Love. We created bombs to protect the things and people we love from other people we fear. Love is a limitless, ever-expanding powerful transformative force. This love holds no conditions, so it never turns to hate or fear. It won't leave you for a younger model when your body gets older and it won't need you to make it feel special.

This loving infinite energy cannot be limited to one person. It isn't exclusive, it is abundant. This love knows only complete acceptance of all, as this love is everything. We are Love and Love is us. When we consciously get in touch with us as a creative representation of Love we have to show love in its physical creative form everywhere. We then start to give and show and tell the world about the Love we are. When we know we are Love, we see the love in others, as if a light switch in a dark world has just been turned on and we see what we have been looking for all along was already there.

When we become Love and show that love in forms of creation, expression in forms of loving of ourselves unconditionally, a cosmic shift occurs; when we express ourselves as Love we open the doors to the attraction of love. Not just from the people close to us, but from the very soul of the universe.

This might sound like an idealistic song that John Lennon might have written or a load of new age twaddle unless you have felt it. Being aware and conscious to Love is to be in service of the highest level of good for all involved in your life and moment to moment experience of life. This includes being your authentic-self. Without loving who You are, the true essence of You, and honoring who you are by being authentic towards others you can't fully love them or you. Love then becomes about fulfilling the needs of your ego. This love has limits. Being responsible for your own ego-based love and addressing it as issues arise from your ego's needs transcends us towards the love that understands that we are not separate, that we are one.

So if I love another person fully, than I love myself fully in return. Love is an infinite energy source, if I love all I come into contact with, I am also loving myself in the same unconditional way. This doesn't mean if someone is treating us badly we must have a 'love and light' forgiving attitude, it is our Loving responsibility to show them that their behavior is out of line with Love. We are not allowing them to grow by learning from their mistakes, this doesn't serve the world; Love is a commitment to another person's growth which brings about your own growth in return.

If someone is being nasty we can tell them that's how they are coming across from our ego; this may result in a damaging argument but if we tell them from our Love it will allow acceptance and love. "Your ego is being an asshole right now, and I love your spirit anyway."

Understanding this kind of conscious Love you have two options. Firstly, being in love with one person, and with that person, working though your ego-based wants and needs to become the best person you can be. The relationship has wings, you can grow together, you are both in service of that growth of each other towards pure love and acceptance of them which leads to an acceptance of yourself. The second option is to know yourself and understand that you maybe a person who needs to grow through experiencing lots of people's creative expression of their own love. You might find your need to grow cannot be limited to one person in this lifetime and that many lovers or friends are needed for you to feel full and whole as a person. More and more people are finding through the need to express oneness they can't limit themselves to the 'special' relationship of just one.

Ego-stroking love

We all love having our ego stroked from time to time. Being told we are beautiful or how wonderful we are. When we love someone else we often love how that person makes us feel about ourselves. Therefore we love us when we are around them; this is a form of ego-based love. Our lover builds our self esteem; it can become addictive as we enjoy the rush of being such an important and integral part of someone's life. This can even work on a mutual basis where both partners feel great when loved so fully by the other. Being in love with the feeling of being loved isn't the same as loving your partner. It can be hard to tell the difference, as the emotions and the addiction can be so strong. As soon as the loving complimentary partner is having a hard time and unable to be so attentive the gap becomes very obvious. This can bring out feelings of being abandoned and unloved; the panic can set in that the relationship is failing as the once ego-stroked lover feels abandoned and unable to support the giver in their time of need. In a sense this relationship is based on emotion use and support. When the support of one is missing the other feels short-changed rather than stepping up their level of support.

One may be the user as they have a feeling of being useful and enjoy being the person who helps and the other. This may make them feel worthwhile and give them a purpose. The other may enjoy the compliments and being the center of someone's universe. When this codependent balance is broken the relationship losses its balance and can fall. This can be through one no longer needing the other, or one going through a hard time and needing more than is being offered.

Most relationships start with ego-stroking love, the collection of compliments from the ideas of 'you complete me'. It may then build into sexual lust-based love which often burns itself out. It can also be emotional love which ebbs and flows as it is love that has conditions. For long term these relationships won't survive unless built upon with a different kind of love, conscious love.

Conscious love!

To be conscious you must be aware of yourself and your motivations, be willing to act against certain ego states to be able to love fully, be aware of your fear, your Pain Body, and your ego sub-personalities. When you are conscious you question the motivation behind your own thoughts, actions and intentions and not those of your partner. You work hard to be mindful of yourself and of the actions and reactions you are making within your relationship. We also need to view all aggressive acts as a cry for love. It doesn't mean we have to put up with all kinds of nonsense, but bring your love rather than your own Pain Body and ego. Sometimes the greatest, most loving gift is to walk away and give the highly spiritual lesson that spells out clearly that the person needs to change as their behavior is unacceptable for the growth of a loving relationship.

Consciously acknowledging the origins of your actions on a

subconscious level is vastly important, but not always easy to do. We are used to projection outside of ourselves, feeling that the issues and problems we are having come from some external force that needs fixing. It is often, if not always, the perception of our own suffering which is at fault. That perception in relationships is likely to come in the form of blame for our unhappiness on our partner for not fulfilling what we need, emotionally, sexually or practically. When you shift your consciousness from your perceptions onto your inner dialog with yourself, a shift happens and we stop blaming the external world, take full responsibility and change our emotions.

People may go through a number of marriages and find that the same stumbling blocks occur as the common denominator for the problem is present, which is Them. This is what is moving from one relationship to the next. It is easy to say, "Well all men or women are like this," rather than realizing our own behavior inspires how other people act. When we change ourselves even in the smallest way, shift and change happens.

> The problems that face us cannot be solved at the same level of consciousness that created them. What we need is a shift in consciousness.
> Albert Einstein

Collective consciousness

Consciousness isn't restricted to the 'self'. We often think that consciousness is something that goes on inside of the mind and that is in the brain inside of our skulls. However, if you take a moment to try and listen to where your thinking voice is coming from, does it feel like it comes from your head? When you have a vision from your imagination, where does it seem to come from? Or when you remember a scene from your past, does that come from inside of your head? Do you see the vision in your eyes? There is no right answer to these questions as it's based on your own perception and the results might vary widely. Most commonly we see conscious thoughts in our head but some schools of thought say the subconscious is in within the body as a whole. We also have a Collective Conscious Mind, which is now only starting to be fully acknowledged scientifically. For example the steam engine was invented by several unrelated people in the same few weeks. The most famous story of collective consciousness is that of the hundredth monkey:

In 1952, scientists were watching monkeys in the wild. They were providing them with sweet potatoes which got dropped in sand. The monkeys liked the taste of the raw sweet potatoes, but they found the dirt unpleasant. Until one Monkey started to wash the potatoes in water; this was then copied by other monkeys. Then something startling took place. In 1958, the scientists observed that the habit of washing sweet potatoes then jumped over the sea. Colonies of monkeys on other islands and the mainland began washing their sweet potatoes. (The Hundredth Monkey Ken Keyes. Jr) From this and other evidence it is believed that when a certain critical number achieves awareness, this new awareness may be communicated from mind to mind or consciousness to consciousness.

Sharing a collective conscious with your lover is a hard one to attain. Many mothers have the gift with their children. Often the longer you have been together the more it 'unconsciously' develops, knowing each other on a conscious, subconscious as well as a physical level. The collective consciousness is that feeling you get when you know something is wrong before the phone rings. It's even when you think of someone and then you bump into them in the street. Full understanding of conscious and unconscious intention builds unconditional trust. This way you always know if the intention is pure no matter what the action.

Super-consciousness

I also believe that there is a super-consciousness. You could describe this as a creative all-loving consciousness, life force or even God. The problem is it is impossible to describe this in words. The moment you put words to this '....' you have limited it into an understandable small concept. So all I can say is this, it is possible at times to reach this expanse of 'all that is'. It is possible for moments to be in connection to this feeling. Many people try this through meditation, or drugs. I believe this is what we are looking for in everything we do in life; that lost feeling like something is missing that we all feel (I have never met anyone who didn't, so call me if you don't!). We seek it in our purpose for living and we seek it when in love in each other's eyes, I also believe you can find it there too. I don't know how long we keep it, and for me it's not just in one special person's eyes, 'the one' we are seeking to be our life's partner, it's in everyone's eyes. I also believe you can find that 'joining with all that is' by joining with a consciousness of creation through sex; by having sex we create new life, by feeling the highest and the lightest vibration of pure love we attain to feeling the very vibration of God.

Part Four: Consciously facing our sexual judgments, curiosities and sexual ways of life

To be in your intuition is to be able to be mindful of your own process. To understand what decisions come from fear and which come from love. To know when our past teachings are inappropriate to our current thoughts and which ones are correct. To trust our inner guidance and let our judgment rest.

We don't have to live anyone else's way of life to understand them. We are able to understand love and the many forms of love conceptually. Yet we live in a world where people will not let others live and let live. This isn't something that just affects other people, we all have this inside of us no matter how open-minded we think we are or how spiritual we think we may be. The ego wants us to create divides and it will find anyway possible to do that, because if we stay divided the ego can live on as a powerful guidance of our lives; our fear becomes our inner guidance system. When we see our own light in people we thought different to us, then we become guided by love. Last night I watched the Oscars award ceremony; it was mentioned by one of the winners that there had been protesters outside the awards boycotting and demonstrating against the film 'Milk', which has gay subject matter. I felt my body surge anger towards the protesters. This is the same anger they feel; it's also the same anger my gay friend Richard has against lesbians having sex as he says 'it's twice the stuff I don't like.... vaginas.' Love is just love, all love is good love, you can't have bad love, by its own definition, Love is love.

Sex with the same sex
We live in an exciting time where people are becoming more able

to love who they want to love in an enriched open society. We still have a long way to go before same sex partners will be fully accepted around the world, but progress is being made. For me, this will come quicker with a shift in consciousness to embrace love over judgment and fear. This means a certain amount of ego diminishing and enlightenment. The information in this book is accessible to any sexuality, but I wanted to discuss in this section of the book more unusual relationship dynamics. Being gay is not unusual, but it is still a minority, but less of a minority than you might think. Many people experiment with same sex partners without giving themselves the label of being straight or gay. Therefore the lines between what is seen to be straight and what is seen to be gay are becoming blurred. This means putting people in an identification box is becoming rightly more difficult. We are beings of love if we choose to be, and we can be open to love in any form. Why wouldn't we want that?

The people who seem to still need to have an identification sexuality label are those who are 'out gay and proud'. It is important for those who have had to suffer social dogma for their sexual identity, and fight for acceptance in society, need to not hide who they are sexually. Therefore if you want to play gay, but not be gay it is looked down upon by the gay community. This is understandable as it often leads to heartache. For a lesbian getting involved with a woman who is bi-curious, the chances are she will have her experiment and go back to her boyfriends or discover she is gay after all and want to experiment with other women and make up for lost time. It can be a lose-lose situation, which has caused a kind of prejudice from gay people to openly bi-sexual women and men. This can be the same for men too, although it is more likely for woman to be open to experimen-tation.

People often don't want to put themselves in a bi-sexual box if this is the first same-sex lover and yet they can hardly fall into the straight box. So their choice is no box at all and to be described as a person who is in love with another person. Therefore you are described as a person in love, and the sexual orientation of who you are in love with isn't important. We live in a time where people born women can change and become men and visa versa, lines are blurred more than ever before and we need to be open to how amazing love is and not restrictive gender stereotyping.

So why do people want to experiment with lovers of the same sex? This is often sought after more by women than by men. A woman might long for the gentle feminine touch of a woman. Knowing that one woman often knows how to pleasure another woman in very tender ways. Women are often happier to be identified as bi-sexual than men, as there is less social stigma, and therefore more open to experiment. I have understood from many men who are straight that they are happy to have a blow job from a gay man but won't get involved with returning the favor or any other sexual antics. To them this doesn't mean they are bi-sexual, just a fan of oral sex. It seems to be still a taboo subject for many men. This can also be for more practical reasons: the fear of anal sex. Anal sex can be dangerous in a number of different ways. Sexually transmitted disease is one of them. Even with a condom you are not totally safe from HIV infection. Condoms are more likely to break during anal sex than with vaginal sex, due to a smaller less-lubricated entry point. The walls of the anus can also be stretched and rip or split. There is also the poop issue which often puts people off. You are also not as in control being the receiver rather than the giver. It seems to be a lot to deal with for a bit of sexual experimentation.

A man and a woman in a relationship generally are more likely to be joined by another woman. Often women, more than men, choose to be the third point in a relationship triangle which can move from one couple's bedroom to another. This may become a lifestyle choice; rather than being in a relationship with one person they can share others' sexual connections. There are plenty of websites with couples listed crying out for this kind of woman. It isn't as easy for men, however, but it does happen; a male friend of mine was propositioned by a couple in a sauna.

Having a threesome can involve a great bout of excitement and anticipation. It helps if you aren't friends with the third person involved as this may cause jealously and confusion in your current relationship. Often couples who have invited in a third person often find that their intuition with each other becomes stronger. They seem to hold an emotional conversation through telepathy, because of things they can't say to each other in front of the other person. This aspect can bring the relationship closer together; however, at the same time being able to tell that your partner finds the other person more interesting than you can hurt. The understanding is that they will, after all you are someone known, and they are unknown, which makes it more electrifying. You might not even notice, as you'll find the third person more sexually intriguing yourself. In order to have a successful threesome experience, boundaries need to be drawn up before you start. It really helps you decide who is going to be the point of focus. With two women, is the man going to be the point of focus or one of the women? Again this goes the same for two men and one woman. In this situation keeping your intuition open to make sure everyone is comfortable is so important. Often in any group situation a person won't want to speak out if the other people in the group are enjoying themselves; in a sexual situation this can lead to feelings of abuse after the event, during the event you may feel you just don't want to rock the dynamic even if you're not enjoying it. This doesn't help anyone, you need to be happy so all parties are happy during and after the event. There are ways of stating your needs without rocking anything if you are intuitively mindful of others in any sexual situation.

Finding your Gaydar

A Gaydar is the understanding that gay men and women are able to tell using intuition when someone they are attracted to is also gay. Using photos of people who identified as gay or straight all dressed exactly the same with no make-up or accessories, researchers asked gay people to spot which was which; the results were better than pure chance, proving that gay people do have an inbuilt intuition for picking partners. My theory on this is that everyone has this intuition, when we developed language we lost so much of our natural skill of intuition but it becomes stronger when it needs to be used. A bit like if you lose one of your five senses another sense will become stronger, if you can't ask someone out on a date because of some social taboo, your intuition will become stronger to compensate. This must have been vital in Oscar Wilde's time when you could be put in prison for being homosexual.

Sex with another woman

Women seduce other women much in the same way as they will seduce a man. So if you want to pull a woman the same rules of flirting apply.

When it comes to the bedroom the first thing you will notice is how soft everything feels. Kissing can be really gentle or passionate or hard, but the lips are often softer and obviously the skin lacks stubble!

You are also likely to take it in turns to pleasure each other. One giving and one receiving, obviously this can be shared in the same way heterosexual sex happens; but for a woman with a woman, there is no obvious stop point. After a man has achieved an orgasm and his brain has become flooded with sleepy chemicals it is unlikely for sex to continue. For two women you can go on and on and on! So you really have to read the subtitle signs and be intuitive as to when your partner has had enough or just for you to be honest when you're ready to throw in the towel!

Intuition remains stronger for women, so it's likely that sex between two women will be an intensely emotional connection.

There are exceptions to every rule and many of us women who are more masculine or dominant.

Why lesbians fall in love deeply; Louise's view

I should preface this by saying that there are always exceptions to every rule and I believe that until recently I was an exception and I was more masculine in my approach. Years of therapy have finally paid off!! I think that men experience orgasms in their penis and their connection with their partner goes about as far as that, literally any hole's a goal. If their willy is stimulated and happy with that stimulation their brain finds it really hard to overcome that, which is why they are lead by it and sex is just sex to them. It goes no deeper. Women have orgasms in their whole. That's not a spelling error; I mean the whole of their selves. So their minds, their bodies, their hearts, and to have ultimate orgasms for most women you need to tick all the boxes; this then sets up a paradox that if a woman gets an amazing orgasm they must have connected with their partner on all those levels to achieve it and they then tend to fall in love with the provider of it. This happens regardless of the actuality of the circumstance.

Sex between men

I asked a very good friend of mine who when I first knew him was heterosexual, what the differences are between making love to a woman and making love to a man. I was also curious to ask what process he went through in his life change to become a gay man. Here is his response:

At the ripe old age of 22 on sleeping with my first man, I often told people it was the first time and I had never thought about it (being gay) before. In retrospect that was true but – (and it was definitely the first time I'd slept with a man - I'd been too much into girls before to stop and think of alternative sleeping arrangements) but I must admit "feelings" had been around a long time. However, coming from a small-minded town and having red-top tabloid reading material at home, homosexuality never appeared on my radar. That was apart from performers around at the time, such as Boy George (no, I was not interested in him) and then in my mid-teens I found some gay porn! That said, growing up is weird and even on watching it (and finding it arousing) I still never thought of myself as gay at the time.

I'm not sure why. I still think it is the mixture of small-minded hometown (i.e. a pressure to conform), red-top tabloids (being gay was ridiculed in the 80s), etc. Whatever it was, what I still find odd today is that I made sure I was 18 before I lost my virginity to a woman – and very lovely she was too (and still is). We were roughly the same age, she slightly more experienced than me and it felt like the most normal thing in the world. I can't say I was doing it under duress and it certainly sparked my interest in straight sex for the next 4 years or so. Why I'd waited so long made no sense!

In my late teens, I did kiss a few boys and it was nice! But it never went any further and was usually drunken challenges on nights out in the local town. I have since learned friends at that time "knew". I just wished they'd told me! Actually, I am glad they didn't as I made some really good friends over that period and beyond Some were girlfriends and some weren't but a lot of us are still friends today and that may not have happened had I slept with a man earlier.

So, to that point: On sleeping with my first man and for a short while after, I still did not really consider myself "gay". I was back in the small-minded town, the red-top tabloid was still on the kitchen table and girls were still finding me attractive and me them! It was very strange. What I do remember distinctly were all the feelings of that first night as if they were yesterday. Should I/shouldn't I; excitement; terror; anticipation and beauty. The answer to the question I was asked in this story really relates to my last verb, "beauty". Happy to go into brief explanations of the former verbs later if I am asked to but let me jump to the latter to explain it.

I awoke first the morning after. We had not had full sex but waking up to this man made whatever had happened the previous night feel acceptable. It was dawn, very sunny and the curtains were open and I don't know how long I spent just watching his body rising and falling through breathing and sleep, just thinking about everything that a few hours before had taken place. And it felt "right". I watched his body breathing for ages and in the increasing sunlight it had a beauty that made me ask for the first time, "am I?"

I became a bit weird then for a while. An affair started, I didn't tell my Mum (who I had been very close to and still am, so felt very guilty), but on the relationship lasting only a short while, I tried to go back to relationships with woman. I say tried, it didn't work. As much as I wanted it to, something was saying inside that I needed to make a decision. I tried to be bisexual but that too didn't feel right and being close to other gay men, either sexually or flirtatiously, felt good. So I made my choice and have never looked back and now I have been with my long-term life partner between 6 and 7 years and I am the most content I have ever felt with myself (and another). So I guess this is the answer to the question on the difference in energy and vibe is subtle and part of a journey and there is a beauty in it now and the first time. I became and am content with who I am. My family know, my friends know and being with a man, and a man that I love, feels very beautifully natural.

Expansion of convention for growth

I have written this book in the expansion of the convention of the idea of meeting 'the one' and spending the rest of your life with that person. I think that is wonderful if it continues to lead to your personal growth and expansion of love. However, I also want to leave open the idea of growth and the expansion of love though the meeting of many minds throughout a lifetime. Convention doesn't fit everyone and the need to conform limits our growth. Intuition allows us to know who we will work best with on our next growth spurt. It allows us to make safe connections with people who will nurture that growth in a same unconditional love.

Polyamory relationships

Polyamory is having more than one loving, intimate relationship at a time with the full knowledge and consent of everyone involved. A successful polyamorous relationship relies on trust, compassion and love. This isn't the same as allowing your partner to cheat on you. The difference being that no one in the relationship lies and they remain within negotiated boundaries of that situation. It could be that one person in the relationship is monogamous while the other one has another partner or all three could have another partner or all three could be with the same partners. Whatever works is the important factor and these relationships only work with honesty and boundaries. Any relationship, even friendships, exists within a framework of parameters that allow the people involved to feel that they can know what to expect.

Compromises are required from everyone involved. This may especially be true of the monogamous partner. Everyone involved will have to adapt to a completely new way to approach relationships. It may contradict the way you have always believed relationships are supposed to work. Often feelings of insecurity, jealousy and hurt come up for the monogamous partner and for the poly partner they need to work extra hard to keep both partners feeling secure. Being mindful of this while still being compassionate and respectful to any new person who may join your relationship is tricky.

Being polyamorous is not necessarily a choice. Polyamorous people don't choose to be poly in the same way that Gay people don't choose to be gay. This is not the same as someone choosing to have sex with various partners and claiming to be polyamorous to be able to get away with disrespectful behavior. A poly person does consider the needs of those involved, not just their own sexual desires.

Being open to a polyamorous relationship is a real test, but it is also an interesting road to grow spiritually. To be willing to show a lack of ownership over a partner and also an ability to release and surrender your own feelings of insecurity at the same time showing unconditional love is an amazing balancing act. If done well then levels of the ego will be surely challenged and hopefully dissolved. This isn't just a growth test for one partner but everyone involved.

Mitch's polyamorous relationship story

I am a gay woman who has been in a relationship with a married woman for the last six years. It doesn't sound like it should work and it doesn't sound like everybody should be happy but it does and we are. We first met via a mutual group of friends, I knew from the outset that she was married and her husband also knew about me. Nobody was being deceived and I think that is the initial key; I went into this relationship with my eyes wide open and we had already established strong communication and honesty with each other. Now I would like to clear one thing up before I continue. I have become very good friends with her husband, and we do not sleep together. I have no sexual relations with him in any way shape or form, and no, he doesn't watch!

I also can't speak for my girlfriend in this piece, or her husband; I can only talk about how this works for me.

We don't live together, although we do try so see each other as much as possible which isn't always easy when she has a weekday job and I work 24 hour shifts; it can be lonely at times and with shifts it can sometimes be a week before I see her.

There is no jealousy in our relationship and I believe it is because we have always been open and honest with each other. I am faithful to her and I don't feel that I need to own her, or be in her pocket every second of every day. In fact that would probably be too stifling for me; we have our own interests as well as shared ones. Most importantly we have kept the essence of who we are as individuals.

Although I love my independence, we don't live that far apart and I know that should I need her for any reason any time of the day or night she would be there in a flash, and she has been. We talk to each other every day and we make the most of the time we have together. She has said to me that she would climb a chimney stack to get me the top brick should I want it or walk over hot coals for me, and I don't for a second doubt it!

In a way I have my cake and eat it; I have my independence and at the same time I am part of a loving relationship, I am not dependant on her yet I can depend on her. I have grown as a person since we have been together and she has been there for me when I have needed her in some difficult times. I am sure she knows that she can depend on me and that I am there for her when she needs me.

Her husband has, as I have already said, become a great friend. He has also helped me out on big decisions and been there for me. He takes me as I am and has become an important person in my life. We do many things as a group of three but equally the two of us will go out for a meal or go on holiday together and spend time alone.

She has become my best friend and my lover and plays a

huge part in my life. We disagree with each other but rarely argue. She is there when I have a big decision to make or have just had a rubbish day at work. She is loved by my family and my friends and quite simply she is loved by me.

Anna's insights on Polyamory:

I have two friends, one gay and one straight, who successfully navigate the polyamorous world. Both have a primary significant other who connects with them emotionally and sexually, and both engage outsiders in sexual encounters.

There are specific rules on this front. In most cases, they engage outsiders on a one-time basis, and the outsiders are often out of state; oftentimes, names aren't even exchanged. If there are occasions where they find themselves getting too involved, they cut the tie at once. In this way, the primary partner feels no threat to the long-term stability of the emotional/sexual connection.

Significantly, both friends have engaged in polyamory from the outset – these ground rules were collaboratively established at the very start of the primary relationship.

So, I have no problem with polyamory in theory – the difficulty is the ease with which it can shift and become a manipulative experience.

Part Five: Can Kinky Sex be spiritual or is just about ego gratification?

Intuition can tell us if our inner sexual drives are healthy or based on self-harm. We can know if we can be free to be creative and play in the bedroom without harming the fragile emotions of our partners and playmates. Intuition can tell us just how far we may go...

The need for the polarity in the bedroom between the masculine and feminine energy is vital. It is the most important dynamic for having sex, even more important than the need for love to have sex. You can have sex and be really angry with each other, but if you have grown to be too much alike in male and female vibration then the polarity of vibration is lost and so is the turn-on.

What some people view as kinky sex can be a way to get back the sexual bite in a long-term relationship. Not just because it is trying something new, but also it often has the male and female energy within it.

A masculine 'doing, fixing, sorting, achieving' woman in everyday life may love to not have to take the lead in the bedroom and allow herself to be ravished or she could be served like a goddess or controlled by her captor with her hands tied above her head. A man who has lost his masculinity can be forgiven when he has no other option than to obey his mistress. This isn't role playing; this is being an aspect of yourself that you know you are, but allowing it to come out and for that to be 100% OK. Anyone who believes that they don't have this side of themselves is in denial of their biological nature. We all have the male and female energy within us and we all like to embody those roles in different ways. Anything seen to be kinky is often coming from not conforming to the sexual identification role you are 'meant' to be. Women are submissive and men dominate. When you look at men and women in everyday life we can see that this standard isn't true, so why is it seen to be true in the bedroom? It might sound hard to believe that the people who indulge in non-conforming sexual activity are normal in today's society and those who partake in what's seen as normal sex are abnormal. This can be a whole range of different sexual pleasure, but when we think about 'kink' we tend to focus of the more extreme examples.

The media puts more sexually kinky TV shows on late at night on cable. With normally a scoffing presenter looking at the out of shape weirdo in the PVC face hoods. It takes us to an extreme of kink rather than seeing a view in the middle which is where most of the population of sexually-active people are. In my time talking to many clients who feel comfortable with expressing who they really are in their sexual preference and fantasy, enjoying their 'dark side', often they feel unable to show their partner, due to social stereotyping. Even some pastimes as simple as viewing porn can lead to insecurity for a female partner. Dildos and vibrators can sometimes lead a man to feel inferior if his partner was to bring them out during sex.

Life is made of opposing forces that work almost in harmony with each other. To have a true value and understanding of what anything truly is, you really need to understand what it is not. We often learn what we do like by having an understanding of what we don't. So if the information in this part of the book doesn't resonate with you, you might like to think it over as a concept to discover why and learn more about yourself. This so called 'dark side' could be the light that saves a long-term relationship. I have decided to include some of the spiritual aspects of some kink that are viewed upon as being the more debase. Looking for personal pleasure and gratification of the self is seen as ego. Wanting to give to another person is seen as spiritual, so all sex can be ego or spiritual depending on your wants and needs. This being the case then there also must be spirituality in kinky, perverted and darn right dirty sex. No matter if it's with a stranger or a lover it is worth exploring to find if this can also take us to break down our judgments and open our intuition, explore ourselves and give to one another.

In this book I am only dealing with consensual sex; intuitively knowing that he or she 'really wanted it' will not stand up in a court of law! I won't even entertain that idea as being sex. Even though the act of rape is sex, it isn't sex. It is violation of a person's free will. The greatest gift we have is free will, free will to live and choose how we wish to live. The idea of handing over your free will to the dominance of another person is a turn-on. Having it taken away from you isn't.

Intuition for kinky sex

In the western culture our new found semi-sexual freedom is moving into more and more different dynamics of possible sexual play. This means that for some their 'Gaydar' is becoming more finely-tuned based on their sexual orientation and fetishes being looking for. This can make finding a sexual partner with the same 'kink' dynamic as you very important. What's one man's pleasure is another man's sick perversion! Making a verbal suggestion during sex that your partner would find off-putting could end the sexual encounter right in that moment, and possibly a relationship too. Using intuition to be able to assess what your partner feels comfortable with and what they don't is important. You could try making a move in that direction, for example a slap of the hand, or becoming submissive, and read the energy level to see if there is an increase in being turned on. How quickly do they respond? In conversation, you may like to make a joke or comment on this kind of sexual activity and feel how their energy changes in the room. Opening your awareness to your partner, rather than saying what you have to say and then closing down for fear of a negative rebuff. Not being open can lead to resentment or wanting to find other sexual partners. Setting out who you are at any point in the relationship is beneficial long term to your own sense of self, balance and honesty.

Types of Kink

Shoes

Shoes are a great way to bring back the feminine energy when a woman has had to adapt to more her masculine side. Women are known for their obsession with shoes. However, shoes fall into two categories of sensible footwear and sexual footwear; although a night out on the town may see a crossover from one to the other. You might not think that shoes are sexual; after all they are closest to the dirt on the ground. But let's consider the humble stiletto shoe.

It has a pointed toe; women point their toes when they have an orgasm. The tall heel representing the erect penis. Walking on a heel means the calf, thigh and buttock muscles are tense, showing more of a curve and muscle tone. The shoe can also have a hint of toe cleavage showing what looks like the cleavage of the breast or bottom. The woman on this ridiculous mode of footwear is also rather vulnerable as she can't run in them, therefore easy prey, except for the fact that she walks with the stride of a goddess (hopefully). Then there is also the dominance and submission of the shoe. An open shoe from the leg to the toe is a powerful dominant woman.

A tie across the ankle depicts a touch of bondage especially is there is a buckle on the strap. It also means that for a man to remove the shoe he must worship at her feet to take it off.

A tie going across the foot is a school girl naivety of not wanting the shoe or her clothing to be easily removed, enticing the more ambitious seducer.

Boots also have the same sexual calling. Thigh-high frames the vagina in the same way that stockings do and gives the impression of sexual power.

Knee-high gives an army-like control where the woman calls the sexual shots with or without heels.

Ankle-high with a heel is a playful tease whereas flat ankle-high is classed as sensible footwear.

Color of footwear:

Shoes should always link somehow with the clothing, however in an all black or dark color then a shock of a bright show gives great attention to the feet.

Red	As the film 'Kinky Boots' says, red is the color of sex. Red hot passion
Blue	Laid-back cool attitude
Black	Sexual and goes with everything
White	Innocent and carefree, up for a one night, doesn't care if it gets damaged or dirty
Purple	Independent thinker
Green	Best left to wellies
Brown	Classic lady in leather
Yellow	Look at me!
Pink	Girlie and optimistic
Orange	If you can buy orange shoes, you're welcome to them!

Footwear is indeed sexual and some people may find themselves having a fetish for footwear or the feet that go inside them. There is after all something we consider to be dirty about feet and whatever we find dirty we also find sexual. This could be due to the position of the sex organs to our behinds and the mess that comes out of any orifice, is sometimes called 'dirty' as we are growing up.

Watching sex in mirrors

Everyone has heard of the idea of having a mirror on the ceiling above your bed with the idea of watching yourself having sex to be a turn-on. This is more so for men, as men are very visual when it comes to sex. Women tend to be more self-critical about their personal appearance and don't get as far as noticing their performance. Any woman who tries on an outfit in a shop that has mirrors all around and bad lighting will often not get past being naked and looking at themselves in the new all view of their backside and not even trying on the outfit. This also means she won't get turned on when her head is thinking and engaged with her body image.

Using mirrors is a great way to give eye contact from a distance, especially if looking at each other when you are so close makes you feel a bit odd. Sitting together and watching each other admire each other's bodies while body gazing in the mirror might be very arousing for some and a nightmare for others. Often our male partner will like their partner's female body more than she does, so try sitting together while he compliments her and shows her what he loves; this is a very strong confidence builder and erotic at the same time.

Mirrors at the end of the bed don't promote a great night's sleep. The spirit as it leaves the body to go on its nightly journey can see itself in the mirror and in shock jump back and then therefore wake up its host body. With mirrors on the ceiling it's not likely to get up.

Film recording

An alternative to looking in a mirror is to film yourself; quite a few celebrities have fallen into the drama of the images being given to the media and broadcast on the Internet around the world. This is no surprise and you may think that no one would be interested in your home movies, but, in truth, what for you is a keepsake of the love you have for each other in anyone else's film collection is porn! So look after it. The exhibitionist would possibly love the idea of someone finding the recording, so for them this is a great turn-on. The reality for the other party may be different; boundaries should be set. With technology as it is through our phones we can send video, photos and voice smut anywhere in the world, but once it's out there it is hard to retrieve.

Filming can be a great way of letting your partner know what you like; you can tell them, while watching, how much you enjoyed a particular act. Just make sure you don't leave it in the player when the mother-in-law is due over.

Voyeurism and exhibitionism

Many exhibitionists who liked to be watched while having sex never turn and look at their audience. It is the feeling of being watched that they enjoy. Many of us can feel when there is someone watching us in the street; our intuition tells us so. It is this acute sense of feeling and this attention from sometimes a complete stranger that often feels the most erotic to the exhibitionist.

The voyeur who likes to watch sex taking place, even though they may find it a turn-on may also speculate as if watching art taking place in front of them. It is often not when they are watching, but a good while after that that the excitement from the event turns to sexual pleasure. These events are harmless if done with permission of both parties. Often taking place at clubs and private parties. Sometimes a woodland area or car parking area will be a meeting place for people to watch each other, sometimes through the windows of cars. Of course this is illegal and if you are caught it could be very embarrassing.

Outside in nature

Spending any time in nature can be sexual. Spring and summer is sexual for people as we wear less clothing showing more skin. We also walk differently, more confidently without the heaviness of our clothes. We feel better when we are not cold and the sky is blue. During the spring and summer we pick up the vibration of everything around us making the next generation. Everything feels like it is being born anew, the blossom and the new leaves on the trees; no wonder when we describe talking about sex we talk about the 'birds and the bees'. The weather can also be very sexual; heavy rain and powerful thunderstorms can send a thrill through your body. Making love in heavy rain when it's still warm and humid is very erotic. The hot sun on your back too. Even snow (if you like that kind of thing) is very beautiful and enchanting too. In fact sex in nature is erotic for many reasons; obviously there is the fear of getting caught, which heightens our awareness, making our heart race and allows us to become more sensually aware of what's going on. Obviously having respect for others is important; you wouldn't want a child to stumble upon you, and as it is still illegal in most countries to have sex in public, you won't want to be caught by the police which tends to make it even more tempting. This makes it not only erotic but also naughty too! Allowing the breeze to cool your naked body touching your skin can almost be as sensual as human touch. The feel of grass under you or being pushed up against a great powerful tree means you can absorb the very energy of nature around you. Of course there are many practical concerns: sand gets everywhere, getting caught, sex in water can be dangerous for the woman, poisonous plants and insects and not losing your clothing. One event that still brings a smile to my face when I propositioned my partner at the time to have sex in a secluded area of the beach surrounded by cliffs and caves in Mexico, he said, "It's cold, and we only have 20 minutes!" He did have a very good point but opening our awareness to the world around us while experiencing pleasures through or under our clothing can be the most wonderful feeling.

Dominance and submission
We are not cavemen and women, but our natural drives are still

much the same; the desire to ravish and be ravished still exists. It is our ego and our upbringing that dictates if we follow our need to get truly connected with our sexual passion or if you politely look for signals of sexual interest. As we have discussed becoming turned-on often happens *after* sex has started and not before. Letting your partner tie you up and take control means:

- You don't have to worry about getting anything right or wrong.
- You can let go of your day and any unfinished work or practical concerns as there is nothing you can do about it.
- You can be fully in the moment as there really is nowhere else you can be right now.
- For once in the day you can let someone serve your pleasure and you don't have to be responsible for anyone else's needs.
- You can let go and enjoy in a relaxed meditative state of fluffy seduction arousal and you are able to turn your mind off and your body on.

Pure bliss! But if the control freak in you can't handle the idea you might want to try this. Before the event write emails between you and your partner about what you would really want. Include:

- Names you would like to be called and things said.
- Favorite positions (there are more ways of being tied than your hands above your head!)
- The way you would like to be touched.
- How long the session to last.
- Code word for stop. As often stop can be used in the heat of the moment and not mean stop!
- And any other fantasy role play your heart and loins might desire.

If you are in the flow of a sex session, your partner is being Sub and you Dom and suddenly your partner bursts into fits of giggles and your strong masculine dominant role is being reduced, don't stop. This is often normal; it takes more power to stay quiet and wait for the outburst to stop. If, however, it sets you off into hysterical laughter it can only bring you closer, but it doesn't mean it failed. As a Sub, try not to laugh but sex is about having fun at the end of the day.

Spanking and physical pain

Not everyone's cup of tea, but it has more uses than the idea of causing pain coupled with pleasure:

- It slaps you into the moment in literal sense.
- If you are bent over it gives you an erotic rush of blood to the head.
- It can give you a form of almost shamanic rhythmic meditation that leaves you feeling as relaxed as a deep tissue massage.
- Any part of the body starts healing after pain. I'm not sure if this would get rid of cellulite, but maybe!
- There is an endorphin rush which makes people feel great.
- A blush to all four cheeks.
- The aura is also expanded in the same way it would be after a healing session.

The person being spanked goes off on a bit of a journey. In order to handle the pain they remove themselves out and of their body. Their spirit takes them to a different level of conciseness. This seems to be different to a meditation, something faster to achieve and a totally different level of awareness. This is like a shamanic journeying, where the soul can be taken to different levels of the astral plain. Some people may see visions; some people are just in a total level of awareness.

These states can sometimes be addictive. Its downside is that you will feel like you need a hug after. It can also leave you feeling a bit lost and bring up issues if you were slapped as a child. Many professional dominatrixes will call their clients about three days after a session to check they are OK. Often the person would feel depressed or sad around this time; more on that from Mistress Alexia below.

This is often also the case after a healing session or massage. It is said to bring emotional issues up to the surface. There is indeed a very powerful connection between the submissive and the dominant. Maybe it's the drumming of the repeated sometimes rhythmic spanking, or maybe it's the heightened spiritual trance-like state because of the pain. Something I'm sure must also happen when someone is being tortured. I have heard women describe this separation between spirit and body when they have been raped. Having it in a controlled environment with someone you trust and a code word to make it all stop is a conscious and life expanding experience.

Interview with a dominatrix: Mistress Alexia
In an S & M play session both players are open and clear and know each other's needs. You should know each other's limits, you as a dominant would know your submissive's limits, what they will and won't consent to. The idea of the session is to push each other's boundaries and limits. If it all goes well what you get from it is a great big endorphin high. Often in day-to-day life people don't get this rush of endorphin high.

There are various stages of aftercare. I ask before a session what the person needs. For some people they are fine and ready to rock and roll. For others they feel very emotional and needy. It's important to ascertain what a person requires from the start so you can provide that. For a dominant, after a particularly intense session of play there is what some people call a 'top drop' where a couple of days later you may experience an emotional slump - you may get teary and emotional and have a crash a bit like mild post traumatic stress, some people feel sick, the same can happen for your play partner. It is usually the dominant who manages the submissive's aftercare but in pro sessions I would usually do this by an email debrief. I have played with people who have said that during the scene, things from the past and their childhood have surfaced, things long hidden. For other people they feel that they can never have that intense feeling in the rest of their life and they feel that what happened is something outside of everyday life.

For me as a dominant if I do a really intense scene it requires a lot of emotional and spiritual energy, it's a closed scene intense between two people; a tableau between two people. Everything else in life is excluded. You are the provider. An intense session can be emotionally and physically draining and a few days later I will drop and have an outpouring of emotion. I recognize it for what it is and I pick myself up.

If you have a real connection with someone it becomes more than physical, a dance, a switching of boundaries. One leads for the other to follow and then the other will lead, but this is rare and usually only happens for me if I play intimately with another dominant.

I can beat someone's ass for £250 per hour but for me it needs to be more than that. The scene has to spark my interest. I have to have a connection with the people I'm playing with. For me, SM is steeped in ritual, SM is sadomasochism. There are various facets to what we loosely term SM play, for example, D/S (dominance and submission) may not entail the players being into sadism or masochism i.e. they may not be into giving and receiving pain. Other people may be masochistic but not submissive. They may be into servitude (including domestic servitude), humiliation, objectification and so on.

If I'm with someone I don't normally play with and it's a client I have a ritual.

I will tell them to get ready and leave them alone in a room to reflect quietly; often I will leave them to the point where they think I'm not coming back. During that time I'm getting into the head space and when I put my shoes on, I'm there. When I walk into the room I'm in an altered state, my dominant persona takes over. I check my equipment: check my ropes, lay out my whips. You play it through your head. It's a physical, but emotional connection with your weapons and tools. I might light incense clear the space for that session.

It's the most heavenly feeling, I cannot describe, a mixture of the visual, the ecstatic, the costumes and the heady scent of latex that moves me. I've done scenes in clubs full of people where I have been playing unaware of anyone but those involved in the scene until I have turned around to find there is a club full of people watching. Hopefully, they are all getting the same buzz.

You can't teach someone this, it comes from within. You need a connection but if it's not in your blood it's not going to happen. You can teach technique (whiphandling, shibari [Japanese rope bondage], caning etc), but if the person doesn't have a natural connection you can tell. I have different personalities (Sadistic Mistress, Daddy – which brings out my masculine side); they don't come out in full force during everyday life but they are within my character and appear in a more muted form. To find someone who shares the same connection as you is an amazing experience and a wonderful gift to share.

Lastly, I only endorse safe, sane and consensual play and would never do anything that was outside of my skills – for example, a whip can be a dangerous implement in the hands of the untrained. I also never play with anyone under the influence of drugs or alcohol – that is non-negotiable. www.mistressalexia.net

Clubs

Nightclubs are often the best place to take part in sexual play with another partner as well as your own. This is because there will be less opportunity for jealousy and you are able to walk away without any connection to you or your life outside of the club environment. This world is a closed door for many people, an invitation-only experience. Getting that invitation can come about from joining what's known as a 'Munch'. This is a group meeting of likeminded people, often found on the Internet.

Other less formal clubs such as Torture garden UK (www.torturegarden.com) are easy to get along to but with a strict dress code of uniforms, fetish, rubber and leather. Don't turn up in leather trousers and think you will get in at the door.

What to expect at a club like Torture Garden is a wonderful display of costumed people. I love the idea of dressing up and being someone else for the evening and many people go into real effort for their costume. You will find dance floors and play rooms where you can look upon or take part in being tied to things in the dungeon and paddled. It looks from the outside voyeuristic and done to show an audience of blank-faced onlookers. Who don't even offer an ohh or an arr as the butt cheeks get redder. This is a place where transvestites, straight and gay all have a common sexual interest which somehow unites them even coming from different sexual orientation. Some even cross into the other domains. Straight guys dressed as women, women bi-curious get away with a snog and a feel in the couple's room.

One club I went by myself to talk to the people there. I got chatting to an old man, been married 25 years. Every Easter his wife goes to visit her sister, he dresses up as a woman, and just sits and watches the action in the dungeon. He told me how he wished he had this in his day. It's the only time he feels himself and alive. I thought of his wife, and thought that she possibly does know about this, just doesn't let on she knows. Maybe that is the secret to how long they have been married?!

I also checked out the couple's room. The experience was invigorating; it is a dark room where you can hardly see anything, but you can hear everything. It's a room of mostly strangers having sex; it was so out of normality but so ordinary at the same time.

Cross-dressing

Cross-dressing is more common for a man to dress as a woman than a woman as a man. In fairness woman have much nicer choice of fabrics, colors, textures and designs. Often a cross-dressing man can be heterosexual but enjoy the sensation of woman's fabrics against his skin. The public portrait of men dressing as woman has become more acceptable, from Pop stars in the 1980's to comedians like Eddie Izzard. It can be confusing for the female partners of a man who dresses as a woman to not think that he is gay. However, there are many personal reasons why people cross-dress and for me, why shouldn't you be able to dress how you wish to and break label identification? This is a complex subject and a very individually-based one, and surprisingly often more to do with identity than sex, sexual preference or fetish.

Fisting

An interesting viewpoint on fisting a friend of mine shared with me that I would like to share with you. I have to be honest it's not something I have ever given any contemplation to. So over to someone with experience:

I have never given or received fisting as a part of S&M play; I have never done it with a man and have never done it anally, though all of these things are possible.

All of my positive experiences receiving have been with partners whom I trusted and who listened to me; if this was lacking it just couldn't happen. Occasionally it doesn't happen anyway but this was never meant to be a quickie.

My first experience was receiving and only about 18 months after the canal birth of my second baby, but it is possible to achieve without having given birth, it's just about developing the muscles; my partner was a small woman with small hands. I was completely blown away by it as it gives a very different orgasm. It still rocks my world but you can have too much of a good thing – variety is the spice of life. There was (and still is) an element of pain but it's there for guidance. If it hurts don't do it! If it's uncomfortable push the boundaries till it just starts to hurt, then ease off for a bit and push on again; this helps the muscles to relax into it slowly. And there is the key; relaxation and slowly. The giver cannot rush it. I find it works best when the two are really in tune and the giver reads the responses of the recipient and is completely happy to take guidance. Like all orgasms how they are achieved needs to change in response to my body's desires (which I also know is linked to my cycle). Sometimes it's about the length of the stroke, others it's about the movement inside with the absence of the stroke. It can also be really hard at times (usually around ovulation) or very very gentle and although these different techniques produce different orgasms they are always major ones, which make you feel deeply and utterly connected to your lover.

It's an awesome feeling for the giver too. Your brain can't really comprehend where your hand is, you feel utterly connected because her vagina is holding you, sometimes the penetration can cause an orgasm (usually if she is multi-orgasmic) and you feel her experience this. At all times you must follow her lead; she is extremely vulnerable to injury and however minor it can be off-putting.

When it comes to withdrawal, slow and relaxed is again the key. In all my experiences there is such intensity of emotion at withdrawal that it is important that the giver doesn't just rush off. I think it's because once that physical connection is broken you truly realize what took place and that is overwhelming.

Asphyxiation

An extreme stereotype of this kind of stimulation is to put amyl nitrate (also known as poppers) or isobutyl nitrate in the States on an orange fruit and put the orange in your month. The amyl nitrate dilates the blood vessels and allows more blood to get to the heart, brain and genitals. When the orange is used you can't get quite enough oxygen into the blood. Blackouts after orgasm are common. The idea is to starve the brain of oxygen for a short time up to the point of orgasm, which gives you a harder stronger orgasm. The risk of this is brain damage or death, and we have probably all heard about the famous people who have died in this way. It can happen when the limits are being pushed and something goes wrong.

Zoe's story:

Asphyxiation comes in many degrees; the rest of these don't often make such good headlines but, for me, great sex.

I found the joy of asphyxiation first when having sex lying over the side of the bed, to increase the rush of blood to my head which intensifies orgasm; on this particular occasion just my head was hanging off the bed so when I tilted my head back it meant that my breathing was restricted. I decided to explore this sensation. I learned to hold my breath for a very long time and I now automatically hold my breath when I orgasm to the point where I can get tiny pinprick-type hemorrhaging, similar to that seen in victims of strangulation, all up my neck and on my face. It is best though when I give someone else that control; you just have to feel confident in your partner. A hand around the throat, across the mouth or a pillow over my face or being pushed face down into one; it can even be something as subtle as when my partner is on top, them pressing their hand onto my chest. Anything that restricts my breathing can do it for me; it's not all gimp masks and straws.

Paying for sex

You might be surprised about how many men you know have had sex with a sex worker. You might also be surprised at how many women wish they could. The sex industry gives a valuable service and there are many situations where it will ease a problem:

- Losing your virginity.
- If your partner becomes disabled and isn't able to make love.
- If your sex life has broken down, many women can handle a sex worker over an affair.
- To try out sexual turn-ons you wouldn't want to ask a partner to do.
- An extra person in the bedroom with your current partner (threesome).
- To gain confidence when making love to your true partner.

Finding a large reputable brothel rather than someone off the street is a must. For many sensitive men and women they can become emotionally involved with the life of the person they are having sex with. Make sure as far as possible the person has chosen to earn a living through sex for a nice income and not out of some horrific circumstance. Use your intuition to be sure this person is OK and happy about what they do before blending your energy with theirs physically. It's a difficult scenario for intuition. Most people who seek a prostitute really don't want to be building a connection and you also don't want to know anything about this person's life, past clients or if they are bored silly and wish you would get it over with. Don't allow your libido to convince you that this person thinks you're the best client they ever had. If you need that feeling, use your imagination, but don't tune in. Protect your heart chakra by visualizing you have a silver disk over the heart area if you have a tendency to be an emotional person. Use your discretion and be vigilant, trust your intuition to find the right worker, if you have any doubt, don't do it.

Open mind /open intuition

I'm sure that there is much more I could add to this section of the book and to the individual sections. My intention by including it is just to open your viewpoints up to other thoughts and ideas. They may not suit you, but opening your mind to reading them means you are not closed mentally, which opens you intuitively. When we open our intuition we don't think about being able to hear things we don't choose to. We plan to only open it to things that we want to hear. When you learned to talk you just wanted to communicate. You weren't thinking about the things you might say that will get you in trouble. Having an open mind means things you might pick up intuitively won't revolt, shock or make you judge your partner. When you pick up on something unsaid that you would prefer not to know analyze yourself rather than your partner; it's time to pick up the mirror and not the magnifying glass. Take a look at why your buttons are being pushed. There are some things that may be deal breakers in a relationship, we all have them, but really think about them before you break a relationship over the difference of an opinion that could be based in your fear.

Part Six: When things go 'wrong'

The best personal intuition can never tell you when to let go, the best intuition can never tell you why it's over. Our own emotion can blank out our knowing with the constant questions we don't want answered but, in time, intuition is our healer for the first step in moving on.

It's so important that no matter what happens you stay open to love. This world works on polarities, so keeping open to love also means open to hurt. When you feel like your soul is crushing all you want to do is avoid that pain and never go near it again. Time does heal. I can prove it: if you have ever had a hangover and said 'I'll never drink again' but then you do, or how painful childbirth is yet people have more than one child. In this section in the book we talk about pain, what it is, how to heal and how to protect without closing down.

We all carry an energy system as I described; however, included in part of the energy system is the Pain Body. This is best described in Eckhart Tolle's book *A New Earth*. My own understanding of the Pain Body is an energetic membrane that comes from energy created from our ego when we feel any variations of hurt. As all thoughts create a vibration they all create energy. This dense dark energy sits around you until it is dealt with. We have the opportunity to deal with it often during our lives due to the law of attraction; it draws to it similar situations that caused the pain in the first place. We then find negative patterns forming; the way to clear them is to behave differently in every repeated situation until you find the one that works. A bit like the film *Groundhog Day*, in which Bill Murray wakes up every day to the same challenges over and over. In this way you can identify when the same patterns are coming up in your life. You find yourself with the feeling that this has happened before, but the absolute worst thing you can do is put this down to being 'your luck' and sit back and look for the evidence that the world is unfair to you personally. You might think it's some kind of karma, or it's because you're a nice person other people repeatedly abuse you; but by choosing to buy into the idea that this is just your lot in life you deepen your Pain Body and give a right to its existence in your life. It is difficult to be grateful to such a hard message, but it is only a message telling you about the need for change. The problem comes when we don't know how to change; the easiest way to change is to adopt Bill Murray's approach in the film and take a different decision every time, except, unlike his character, take a different action for the positive!

From my own experience the only way I have ever found to dissolve an aspect of my Pain Body so it doesn't need to keep repeating the message is forgiveness and love. How you create those emotions are up to you; you might want to see a therapist, a counselor or psychiatrist, you may have your own ways of healing, you could just decide to choose differently the next time the same issue comes up.

In relationships you will often find yourself dealing with your partner's Pain Body; they may have reactions to things you say or do which is based in their past and not in who you are being in this moment. When the Pain Body is in full flow it's unlikely a reasonable resolution will be found in that moment; your partner is also unlikely to be communicating from their real-selves. So your reactions to the issue won't heal, as you're only healing the symptoms and not the dis-ease. Take space and return to the issue when the person is back to their normal level of communication.

An ex-partner of mine had a very dense Pain Body; he had been in the army and had a very bad childhood. He would tell me that he was trouble and that I shouldn't bother with him, but for me I could see his potential and the good that was inside of him and I worked hard with him to bring that out. At times he would be winning over his Pain Body and start to become happy, then he would feel guilty about his happiness and the Pain Body would win. In the end I realized the only person I could make happy was me and living on an emotional yo-yo really wasn't going to bring anyone any joy. I took the hard decision to move on. No matter how bad a relationship is, moving on can feel like you failed that person you made a commitment to fix. No one can fix your Pain Body, and you can't fix anyone else's. You can just love and support.

I believe the Pain Body can come with us from one lifetime to the next with the major unresolved issues from that life. A client of mine had a skin condition that meant her skin would swell and small blisters appear. Tuning in using intuition, I found she had been burned to death by members of her family for bringing shame into the family by sleeping with the wrong man. We discovered the blisters came when she felt she couldn't trust someone or was in a difficult emotional situation. Her skin condition didn't flare up again once she had sent forgiveness to those who wronged her in the past life. I'm not saying that it's that easy with everything; we can't always just wave a magic wand of forgiveness for pain caused in childhood or past lives. It's a journey to transform our pain into learning. If it can become positive, we can forgive, as we can't stay angry for something that benefited us.

Unreasonable behavior is often the result of an active Pain Body. If you find you have a strong Pain Body, avoid alcohol; when we drink alcohol we remove our conscious mind allowing the Pain Body to take charge. We all have a Pain Body so it doesn't mean you will have to remain single until you get it sorted, but it can hold you back. Once you recognize the problems of your Pain Body you may ask your partner to help you deal with them and help you recognize it yourself. It's almost impossible for you to see it yourself when it flares up. It's only becoming mindful after the event and doing your best to make amends for any hurt you have caused. Know what your triggers are and knowing how best to avoid them. Everyone has a Pain Body, but you can evolve to make it unnoticeable and healed.

The Pain Body of each person differs in density. If the Pain Body of your partner is too dense and you feel fearful or anxious you do need to consider walking away.

The more forgiveness you practice, empathy, intuition and understanding, the less you will add to your Pain Body. No one else is responsible for adding to it. It's what you make a situation mean to you that will quantify if you add to a Pain Body in a given situation or not.

Anna's experience with her partner's Pain Body:

When I was 24, I became involved with a man who was 36. He had never dated anyone for more than a year; I had only had one other relationship. Within a short while we were furiously in love (or, rather, lust): the sex was incredible and intoxicating, and the fact that we were long-distance only added to the mystique.

As time went on, he began asking me to make rules for what he could and could not do with other people, as his tendency to hop from girlfriend to girlfriend had led him to believe he was 'polyamorous'.

This raised the first red flag in my gut. I wasn't keen on being the only one to set the rules – rules he'd only have compulsion to break, if his previous relationships were any indication.

We settled on a compromise: we were both performers on the road a lot, and I honestly didn't mind the idea of him making out with some rabid fan as long as my health wasn't at risk as a result. The one rule we established was this: Fooling around a bit was fine, but you had to speak up if you were falling for someone else.

About a year into the relationship, we were finally living in the same city, and a few trends began:

First, holding each other at night, he'd tearfully confess he'd never felt so close to someone, and that it was making him feel like running away. His mother had abandoned him and his father when he was a teen, and I knew he had huge abandonment issues as a result.

Second, he became incredibly controlling. He would have angry outbursts at the smallest thing, and he began criticizing my work, ambitions, intellect, etc under the guise of loving me and helping me. It got to the point where I'd arrive at his apartment (he never came to mine) and he'd demand that I stand in the hallway until he was ready for my 'energy'. My 'energy' would be, at times, too loud, too down, too up, too overwhelming, too underwhelming...

Third, he increasingly began pointing out other women and analyzing our relationship with a cruel coldness, saying things like, "I still find you fun and interesting and intelligent and visually appealing, but you are not sexually attractive to me like you were at the beginning. Jane, however, is extremely sexually attractive, and I gave her my number because I wanted to go home with her, but I realized that might be insulting to you."

I met all this with patience, feeling it was my duty to be the Woman Who Doesn't Walk Away; he was an injured child testing me to see if I'd leave him like his mother had.

My gut was in knots, but my brain had OD'd on chemical love.

Finally, just before we were set to move in together, he took a business trip. He met X on a Saturday, took her home that night, and flew home Sunday absolutely thrilled – because he was now in love with two of us, and they'd already arranged for her to come visit.

When I balked at this – our limit had been 'falling for someone else', hadn't it? And didn't I have any say at all in this matter? – he was furious, berating me for my "stupidity" – X had 'nothing to do with us'; she was "totally separate", and I was "dumb" if I was going to break up and miss out on being with him.

Moreover, for my hesitancy, I was being "irrational", "female", and "idiotic".

I finally broke things off – this wasn't polyamory, this was misogynistic polygamy – and he was emotionally unbalanced, distant, and lacking compassion.

When I look back, I can't believe how far things progressed and how much I'd subverted myself before I drew the line – it was just that he presented things to me with such convincing 'logic' that I felt like all the problems were mine. Had I had more experience, I might have gotten out earlier, but I've learned my lessons and am determined to not let anything like this happen again.

Avoiding pain

In an effort to avoid pain we will often do anything. This isn't just the pain that we feel but the pain that we inflict onto other people. It is impossible to avoid pain in our lifetime, either physical or emotional pain. I first realized this when my brother had to have a jab at school, it was the BCG jab and hurt his arm which he complained about. As smug little sister it slowly dawned on me that one day I would need to have this jab too. In my future was a predestined moment of pain. No way out unless I was to kill myself (I was quite a dramatic child) but that would involve pain too. I let go and resigned myself to my future predicament. What's very odd is that when the day came I didn't need the jab as I already had the immunity! When we live life in fear of pain we really stop living altogether. Pain is a fact of life; we need it to be able to understand love. We always need the polarity between love and fear, avoiding one leads to bringing in the thing we are avoiding and means we don't experience the emotion we long for; what we resist persists. The more you focus on the avoidance of something, the bigger the thing you're avoiding becomes. By avoiding pain, we lie, manipulate, and avoid situations or people we really deal with. We live in denial of our responsibilities and can sometimes create a false identity of ourselves in order to live a safe pain-free life. We might create a sub-personality which is an aspect of our ego. We know of the parent, adult and child within all of us but we may also employ an inner ego state of a controller to stop people abusing us. Of course the controlling aspect then becomes rejected by others and we feel pain created in a different way. No matter how we avoid pain, it's like trying to stop a water leak; it just springs up somewhere else until we let the water flow or turn it off. Every avoidance of pain leads to pain. This doesn't mean you have to express your pain to everyone involved, just stop trying to avoid feeling it. Instead, connect with it and understand it fully, then move on from it. Every opening to love is opening to every aspect of love; pain may be something we experience and for some of us we understand love through pain: 'If I hurt I know I really love'. This isn't ideal; often people will say you know the love you had after you lose it, which means we are rating our love by the pain over the loss of it. We can't turn pain off and would we want to? It is a valuable messenger that gives us our guidance through life. Without it we can't know love, but to accept it we let it flow, by letting go and letting it flow we open to love and somehow pain doesn't need to bring us any more messages and like me letting go to my future BCG jab pain, we might never need to feel that pain again.

Creating Sub personalities

Often to protect ourselves from pain we create sub-personalities. Within the ego we have many 'selves'. These are masks or characters we put up to the outside world to disguise our more vulnerable aspect of 'self'. Sub personalities of: the frightened child, the hero, the controller, the pleaser, plus many more. If you have been hurt in childhood you might have an inner frightened child, to protect that aspect you might engage with a controller who keeps people away from the child, by fixing and sorting all situations. But you don't want to look controlling so you have a pleaser who just seems to have no boundaries and is fun and open to everyone.

I see these selves to all be on a bus ride. The bus is on route to the spiritual evolution of the self. All of these sub-personalities are on the bus. I love them all, but I don't let them drive. If my pleaser drove it would pick up hitchhiker boyfriends and take them on their journey and ignore my own. My controller would drive all night without breaks and become a workaholic and my frightened child doesn't feel good enough to sit behind the wheel. Well she is only four! The driver of the bus must be always conscious of its motives and where it is going; as long as the higher self remains in the driving seat I deliver the best of myself to the world. Not always possible but that's the journey of the self – to grow into its highest definition of love and nothing less. Take a look at some of the sub-personalities that might be protecting you from having the relationship of your dreams. Give them another job and get back in control of your bus.

When our past is still living in our future

We are who we are because of the sum total of all of our experiences, however, the events of our past do not define us; the decisions and the meanings we give to our past makes us 'who we are'. If you have had a bad experience, you have a choice to interpret that as something you have grown in wisdom from or something that made you weaker. Through one of the magazines I write for, it breaks my heart to read some of the letters I reply too. In many cases with both clients and letters, I am given a full catalogue of past events going right the way back to being bullied at school. A long list of evidence to prove that life has been really bad to them; which are true, but all these bad events were a message that something wasn't right in their view of life. Changing the perspective, despite the negative evidence, changes life and the way people treat you in it.

There are books about heroes that tell us despite the most horrendous conditions these people have taken the best from it. If you find it hard to move on from events in your past, there are constructive things you can do to transform them into becoming powerful positive events in your life. Your past happened; you choose who it makes you.

The origins of sexual hang-ups

We are born into a relationship and hopefully we are conceived as a part of a loving relationship. That relationship is of course our Mom and Dad. This is the starting point of all of our opinions in life and of people and relationships. Our parents are our guiding force; we learn mostly by copying what we see. An individual's personality is largely formed by the age of five. Therefore most of the events that occur before that time have great meaning. The only problem is we can't remember much of what happened. The decisions we make at this very young age become our map of the world. It is a map which we find ourselves following right through our adulthood.

Neil is a very good example of this: after Neil was born he had his mom to himself for the first eighteen months of his life. She then fell pregnant with his brother and then after her second son was born went out to work. Neil then had nannies, five in all, all with blond hair. All these nannies fell pregnant and left the job of being his carer before their child was born. You may understand why Neil doesn't ever go out with blondes and has a fear of becoming a father!

Although this is a shame for any blond lady with an eye for Neil, it's not such a bad example of what we make things 'mean' from childhood and how we still live by this map. However, if you have volatile patents, who have big arguments, which may even involve smashing plates or violence, who then run off into the bedroom to make love after the argument for a 'kiss and make-up', you might feel that as an adult your sex life is lacking a little spice when you make love to someone. This could even mean that you only feel sex is 'right' when it involves control games or sadomasochism.

We don't think children are aware of sex as it's happening in the bedroom late at night. We must remember from school tales of catching Mom and Dad 'at it' when someone walked into the bedroom, or we remember the occasion when we just knew we weren't wanted around. We are more aware as children, although we might not be able to put a name to what we knew about sex. I guess it doesn't seem important as a child, it's 'grown ups' stuff'. It only becomes interesting when it's a secret. The mere fact it's a secret and there is such a big deal made of it means we build hang-ups about it before we even start having sex.

Nothing else we do as people creates so much attention and judgment and also has so many grey areas. This is largely due to the many influences we have in our childhood, people who have their own issues surrounding this subject; from embarrassing grandmothers who insist on the sloppy kiss, to embarrassed sex education teachers, what we overhear from our parents' bedroom, to your older sister's spotty boyfriend or being called 'lezza' because you go in the school showers naked after P.E. These events shape our tastes, our fantasies, and our sexual preference. The only 'wrong' across the board is anything that forces another's will, or manipulates another's innocence by our intention. Sadly I guess that that would include many of our first sexual experiences.

How many women have heard?
- I'll just sit the condom here on the pillow, in case you change your mind.

- I'll only put it in a bit, to let you know what it feels like.
- I'm too drunk to drive home; can me and my friend stay the night?
- If you loved me, you would.

Don't think that it's only men, women are very persuasive!

- I've had a bad dream, can I get in with you?
- I'm totally up for sex, no strings attached.
- I've never been able to have an orgasm before, but I think I trust you enough.
- I've only had three partners

Our ex-partners can change the way you view yourself and sex. They might have said things to you to knock your confidence; making you feel awful about yourself.

If this has happened to you, you might want to write a list of all of those comments. Then write one of all of the nice things that have been said about you. Always remember it takes two to make a wonderful sexual union. Don't take 100% of any blame!

TV shows can also influence our expectations, making us feel inadequate or even repulsed by sex. Sex really isn't sex when done by actors on TV. We all struggle with belts and bras and annoying buttons and the office desk can collapse underneath you!

We learn through personal experience but our life map, drawn by the influences around us, gives us the first directions. It is up to us to re-draw our experience as we go, so our inner child's map doesn't become our reality of the world, but rather our own personal experience of others. Not what our parents' relationship was, but the potential of something much, much better.

Feeling uncomfortable being touched

If you feel uncomfortable being touched you are not alone. This is a very common problem. Again often rooting in childhood, when as a baby you might not have been held or touched or growing up you might have been touched inappropriately. It's always advisable to consult a professional counselor if this is a real problem for you. Smaller issues can be dealt with in the following ways:

- Start getting professionals to do manicures, pedicures, face massage and eventually shoulder or full body message. This will help you get used to being touched.
- You could start with animals: allowing a dog to lick your hand or a cat to rub against your leg.
- You could draw an outline of your body marking areas in red where you don't like being touched. Then slowly work on these areas with a partner or a friend.
- Ask a partner to help you with aura touching. Close your eyes and your partner moves slowly towards the body to the point where it feels warm or energy can be felt. Touching the aura can be felt as if you are being touched but not on your physical self. Only go as far as is comfortable at first, then a little bit more each time.

If you recognize yourself as someone who feels guilty, embarrassed or uncomfortable sexually, it's important to know the root cause, so you can dismiss it with an adult viewpoint.

Many of us are uncomfortable being touched by strangers, in the form of being kissed or hugged. We are becoming more and more a society of huggers, especially in the spiritual circles. If only more people could be intuitive about when this is appropriate for a person and when it isn't. Let you be the first to set a trend to read others before slobbering them on both cheeks.

Exercises to discover the root of your hang-ups

If you know there maybe some demon in your closet, don't do this exercise; go and see a professional regression hypnotherapist. Try David Samson www.avantihypnotherapy.com in the London UK area

Close your eyes, lie back and relax:

- Think of a moment in childhood when you discovered something about sex or heard someone talking about it.
- It might have just been the feeling outside a bedroom door.
- Take yourself back into that moment and see how you felt as that child.
- Now with your adult's view of the world, what do you think of that situation now and how do you interpret it as an adult?
- Take a moment to forgive the people in that situation and yourself.

Write out your negative viewpoints given to you in childhood and then write a more positive view. For example, some I remember from my own childhood are:

- "All men only want one thing" – I know this isn't true of my brother and many of my male friends. Why would this be then true of my partners?
- "Nice girls don't have sex" – If that was true I wouldn't exist! That would mean my mother isn't a nice person.

Most negative messages from childhood are stored in the subconscious mind. Repeated thought patterns really can change your subconscious conditioning; a great way to do this is through repeating affirmations, such as:

- Sex is a beautiful way of expressing love
- I am a sexual, passionate being and I love that.

These thoughts will filter through and transform the conditioning from negative affirmations you may have been given.

Beware of the voice you have in your mind, and try and transform any negative inner dialogue into positive. Especially don't allow your inner dialogue to become a spectator during sex that will criticize and analyze your every move.

If you feel guilt for sexual pleasure try just enjoying the sensual pleasures of normal life. Take time to really smell your favorite perfume or to wear clothes that have a special feeling for you on your skin such as rich cotton or silk. Do anything that stimulates one of the five senses. As you allow yourself to enjoy, you are giving yourself permission to be physical and enjoying it without guilt. This will rub off on your love life.

Others' sexual judgments and how to free yourself

We live in a heavily judgmental society. A judgment is really an opinion brought about by fear. We believe that it is important to hold tight to our beliefs in how the world should be in order to live the right life. If we truly questioned some of the things we have strong opinions on, we might see that these opinions are not our own, but ones given to us over time that have become our belief structure. Society seems to want everyone to have the same view of the world. This keeps us small and anyone who thinks outside of these small parameters of thought is seen to be wrong. We collectively feel that "what will happen to these people will be wrong in the long term", even sometimes judging people as being bad, because of the way they conduct themselves sexually.

For me sexual crime is taking away someone's innocence, manipulating someone's free will and using force when someone clearly says no.

We still seem to have so much baggage when it comes to our view of sex. Some of this baggage you may even be unaware of. Many people who were brought up in a Catholic household have been brought up with very clear ideas even about masturbation.

One of my friends was sent to see the priest for having a copy of the Sunday Sport in his bedroom.

Breaking these thoughts, however deeply subconscious, can be a liberating experience. Your thoughts create your future; they hold a rhythm and vibration that bring into your life events and people. If you have the viewpoint that all men are sex maniacs that only are interested in one thing, or that women don't like sex, you are likely to meet the people who prove your thoughts to be right. In a sense we manifest all the time without even realizing we do it.

There was a test done for a woman who only met violent alcoholics; she was given a choice of ten possible dates with men behind a glass screen. She chose the only man in the line-up who was a violent alcoholic. She recognized the rhythm of her own father in this man; as this was the first rhythm she was born into, she associated this with relationships and that's the rhythm she was unconsciously seeking.

We then can see perhaps how what we are told or believe about sex becomes the map we use to find our sexual relationships. Changing this map is as simple as changing our thoughts, however, often the thoughts are subconscious.

While having a conversation with a male friend about sexy actresses, I told him that I thought the ultimate in sexy is Angelina Jolie. He replied, "No, she looks like she smells of too much sex." I felt it was an interesting and revealing comment on how he feels about women who have lots of partners, so I asked him. His reply was that he thought men and women were equal and women could do as they liked, but there was an undertone I was aware of that he wasn't. "Women could do what they like, but I won't sleep with a woman who has been round the block." I doubt he was even aware of that thought.

The way to access those parts of your subconscious to see what you are bringing into your life is to feel in your body your reactions to things. I'm going to list some statements and allow your first thoughts to come into your mind, and take the very first answer to the question as the one you believe, but also look for backup in your body. If the question makes you feel uneasy in your stomach or if you feel tension in your chest, these will be indicators to how you judge not just others but also yourself.

Judgments which could keep you limited:

- A woman who has five children by different partners is a tart?
- A woman who has five children by different partners is unlucky in love?
- A man who chats up a woman in a nightclub is only looking for sex?
- A man who chats up a woman in a nightclub is looking for a relationship?
- A woman who wears short skirts is looking for sex?
- A woman who wears short skirts knows she has great legs?
- All men are bastards who are out for what they can get?
- All women are materialistic and like guys with nice cars?

Magazines about celebrity relationships and lifestyles constantly sell us their judgments on the lives of the rich and famous. What are your views really? Can you remove yourself from following the written view and look behind at the person? Or do you tar yourself with the media brush and change your own views and behavior because of what you read. You wouldn't be on your own if you do; recognizing that you do is the first step. Then you need to change your mind. Then you can use exercises similar to the ones for breaking hang-ups to break your beliefs too; repeating affirmations, such as:

- I have wonderful men in my life who enrich and support me.
- I attract enlightened women who understand the deeper

meaning.

Differing sex drives

As David Schnarch said, "In the bedroom, we do the leftovers. After we take away everything that both couples don't want to do, we do what's left."

It's true, but it would be a shame if that were the best we can do. There comes a point in every relationship when you discover what works for both of you and stick with just that. If that goes on too long, the sex will start to stagnate and therefore also the relationship. Sex is 10% of a relationship when it's good and 90% of a relationship when it's bad. When you think how easy it is to have bad sex, I'm surprised that we ever do it at all. There are so many factors to consider:

- For a man: Keeping an erection, cumming too quickly, slowly or not at all.
- For women: Arousal, being able to orgasm, time of the month.

We are not all able to be the Martini girl "anytime, any place, anywhere". Yet we feel the pressure from our society that this is normality when in reality the opposite is true. The person with low sexual desire is always seen to be the odd one out. In every relationship, one person will have less desire for sex; but with a different partner, that person might be the one with the most desire, depending on the partner's desire and desire for that partner.

Suzy's story

Suzy has a very high sex drive. She prided herself on the fact as this was a man's dream, so she thought, as the main complaint when it comes to marriage is that the wife no longer wants to have sex with the husband.

When she got married, for the first year of the marriage the sex life was great. But when he wanted it less and less it became a big issue between them, and then he never wanted it. He was unwilling to talk about it, as he didn't know what the problem was, he felt she was putting demands and pressure on him.

The person with the low sex drive is always seen to be the one at fault, especially if it's the man. A woman will define her self-worth by her ability to be sexually desirable. She may also feel like she is seen as a slut to be the one who has more desire than her partner.

Suzy came to see me as she had now had a few one-night stands, but was still madly in love with her husband. Everything else in their relationship worked.

What the reading showed was that Suzy banked her self-esteem and the love for herself on being a highly-sexed woman and therefore to be wanted and needed by men.

Unknowingly this puts lots of pressure on her husband. Not just to perform as often as she needs it, but her energy towards making love was that of need. Suzy unknowingly was taking her husband's life force energy and becoming a sexual energy vampire. Of course this was very draining for her husband, both on a sexual level but also on a spiritual level. When she realized this she started to look at the way she felt about herself.

She didn't like her own physical appearance, and having sex meant that she felt accepted by her partner. Once she had this realization, she started to look at different ways she could feel good about herself: such as her work and her friends. The small things she did everyday. With the help of a counselor her self-esteem was brought to a level where sex had a whole new meaning for her. It was no longer about reassurance and more about love.

The marriage is now doing great and the sex life is now

healthy for both of them.

Drugs, relationships and sex

It's difficult to escape drug use in our culture. Addiction is a huge problem and as people it is possible for us to become addicted to anything that makes us feel better. This could be from a basic sugar rush or buying something new, right the way through to drugs, alcohol, sex and porn. We can also become addicted to love.

We unknowingly fall in and out of addictions throughout our lifetime; the cause of this 'need' for addiction comes from the different experiences of our day-to-day lives. When we have an addiction we will do anything to hang on to it, even breaking down the quality of a relationship if it gets in the way of our addicted behavior. We may also find people who are addicted to something as serious as drugs very attractive. Drug addicts are often very sensitive people who can see the world for what it is. They've fallen down a gap between reality and our common perception of it, unsurprisingly not feeling they fit in with the world. This may bring out a need in you to heal this person; you may be in love with their potential and not who they really are in this moment. It is also easy to become codependent on the drug user. You may find it's easier to worry about someone else's life than get on with the full potential of your own, often using the addiction of 'but I love him/her'. Not every drug user is addicted; some people do just use them for recreation.

Looking at illegal drugs we see they are categorized into being 'uppers' which make you feel high, happy and able, or 'downers' which make you feel numb or distant.

Hash, heroin, ketamine, Valium are downer drugs, but also they release a feminine energy in your being (passive, stillness, reserving and being). Cocaine, Ecstasy, speed, crack are upper drugs but also they release a masculine energy in your being (doing, fixing, sorting and achieving).

A friend of mine smoked hash everyday because he didn't like himself when he was aggressive or male dominant. He took it as it brought out his feminine side, which he much preferred. He was an artist and he felt that the creative energy of the right female side of the brain was helping him.

Drugs can also be used for attaining a sexual high, such as Ecstasy which is known as the love drug as it gives the same feelings as being deeply in love. It isn't often possible for a man to keep an erect penis when having taken drugs so this may lead to mixing other over the counter drugs such as Viagra to assist. It's very difficult in an aroused sexual state to be aware of what is happening to your body. You may become too hot or lose too many fluids, your blood pressure may become too high or you might blackout, and for the most part it's impossible to achieve an orgasm. Sex on drugs is a big no as it's risky on a number of levels:

- Are you sure you have consent of the person?
- Can you be sure of having safe protected sex when you're not in your right mind?
- Drug are dangerous anyway.
- You might not feel the pain of an injury occurring at the time or be aware of how you're treating the other person.
- Being in a relationship with someone who regularly uses drugs or alcohol when you don't is draining.
- You never know which is the real them.
- You can never trust the emotions as when they're on drugs they maybe very loving and off them they maybe very moody.
- You never know where you stand in their life, but it's always second best.
- The worry of them having an overdose or accident.
- Drugs and alcohol can bring out a violent side.
- They may steal from you or drain you of your finances.

- They could end up in prison.
- You will find yourself lying to your friends and family.
- Would this person make a good parent?
- You spend more time on them than yourself.
- The relationship is unbalanced.
- Hard to get a level conversation.
- Most relationship arguments happen on a glass of wine too many!

The list could be endless. If you are taking drugs with them you may feel overly bonded to this person. There is a very unique feeling when you experience something amazing together; drugs will give you that feeling. But then how can you trust that these are your own true emotions?

Drugs will help you ignore problems within the relationship that you need to address. You will also neglect the important things that you need to do in life. It's harder not to take drugs when someone you are with is using them. Love is never pure in this form, no matter how hard you try loving, and emotions will be based on the need for the drugs and the companion to use the drugs with. Often it's impossible to see the far-reaching effects on our world of drug use; we may buy fair trade coffee and watch our carbon footprint and become vegetarian, then snort coke in a toilet in an exclusive club in Soho. The lives ruined and the death toll to get that white power into a nasal cavity is astonishing. If for no other reason than to make the world a better place, you have to see people who use drugs as trying to expand the love and connection they long to feel, but doing it in totally the wrong way.

In my lifetime I have been in relationships with many people who have been using drugs. It was a form of patterning I needed to break from my own childhood with a father who drank; I have been involved with facilitating a crack and heroin addict to become clean, I have lived with a person who smoked pot everyday, been in short relationships with recreational drug users and friends, dated a man in his forties who took drugs clubbing for long weekends, and inspired a partner to give up cigarettes. I say this to underline a point with my experience. Drugs and relationships do not work, for that matter drugs and life also don't work.

How to know when to walk away

If one person in the relationship says love is broken then it's broken. You have to trust what they are saying even if you believe you know better. It's a basic form of respect.

No amount of you knowing they are a 'soulmate' or that you are 'right for each other' is going to change how they feel. Even if they are lying to themselves it takes great courage to end a relationship knowing you will hurt someone; even if they want to hurt you it means they are so hurt they want to lash out at you and then it isn't looking good. No matter how long you wait or change yourself, no matter how frustrated you may feel or how you know you are 'meant' to be together, you have to respect that they want this relationship to be over. The truth of this moment is the important one, not the maybe of any future moment.

Within my work I have met many people who have gone to see psychics who are little more than fortune-tellers. You might see a psychic who gives you a future prediction telling you that 'your love' will come back to you. This can cause a person to wait years without moving their life forward waiting for this person to come back. The future isn't set in stone, things change. The most attractive thing is a person getting on with their life and becoming happy. It can take up to two years to get over a relationship; that doesn't mean you're allowed two years of needless pining and lack of focus in your life. It just means you're allowed nights when you allow yourself to not do so well and play that song over and over using music as a form of emotional torture. However, if you can make someone wonder if they made a mistake as you are having a great life without them, you stand a better chance of them coming back to you; but you know what, you might just not want them when they do. If a person cannot see how fabulous you are, why would you want to be with them? Even if you are living with regret that you weren't the best of yourself in the relationship, and given a second chance you could do better, if they didn't inspire the best of you, then you can't be the best of yourself. Move on and build your life.

Can't walk away

Walking away from a relationship can happen long before you let your partner know it's time for it to end. Walking away is when you start to end all of those feelings and look elsewhere for what you were getting from that companionship.

People will sometimes stay years in a relationship that they have started walking away from. This can often be because nothing is 'wrong' with the relationship. It just isn't 'right'. People can keep going because there isn't a reason to end, but the relationship starts to unravel, time takes its toll and at some point the words fall from one of the couple's mouths. This is a slow motion break up; almost as if you hear and feel the impact of words you have played and replayed in your head. When they are out on the table there is an unreal quality to the moment and often a sense of relief follows.

I describe this point as the relationship hitting its sell-by date; you know it's going off, but you invested in it and don't want to throw it out, you know if you keep eating it then it will make you sick so you stop eating but hold on to it. Only when it starts to smell do we finally admit it's not just past its best, it's gone off.

We fear being alone. We feel separated from God and we wish to find that sense of peace in each other's eyes. The truth is God is inside of you, that connection to oneness and a sense of completeness is in all of us. Giving you a chance to feel whole is outside of an unhappy relationship not inside trying to make a bad one work. Someone else will come into your life; you just have to know it.

How to break obsessive love

When a relationship has broken down or when we want someone who doesn't feel the same we can obsess over the person. When we are obsessively in love with someone it can feel like we must be going mad and that we are out of control. Sometimes these obsessions can last many years, even without seeing the person you're thinking about. People say that they can't stop worrying, but this isn't true. Worry, like obsession, is formed through habit. These habits can be broken, your mind is a muscle and it can be trained; as you can train any muscle. You can learn to control what you think:

- Allow the thoughts of the person to come into your mind without beating yourself up over it. Let that thought be one thought and not a string of thoughts, all following on from that first thought. Breathe deeply. If the thought continues, replace it with another thought, which can be anything on a positive note.
- Deny yourself the sexual fantasy of this person. If you really want to let them go, it has to be all aspects. Even sexual thoughts about a person create energy and cords.
- Use cord cutting exercises below.
- Keep your life busy with nice things to do and have in your life. Make time for friends. But don't use it as an opportunity to talk about your obsession; it's most probably talked to death.

Life is short; there are so many amazing things to do. Allowing your life to be full of painful obsession is your choice; there maybe something the drama of it that keeps you going back. It could be because you invested so much you don't want to walk away feeling you have lost. What you win is your headspace back, your creativity back and your joy back. Choose a better life for yourself, full of joy rather than pain.

How cords are made and how to break them

When we are curious about a person, our interest, intention, in-depth listening and being heard creates a deep bond. Love is being curious about a person. We also see this in people who stay curious about life and the world; they seem to age less. Staying curious about a person builds love and creates a strong energy bond. As we sleep next to someone our spirits intertwine, our dreams blend and when we are curious about a person's body, physical enjoyment and soul we really open up to a meaningful connection. This connection is in a form of energy cord that runs out of a person and into the other person; they are like umbilical cords of energy. Some people can feel them; they come from the solar plexus. Often people describe this as a physical sensation, and that physical sensation can be described as love. That really is exactly what love is: Love is energy between two people.

I can even tell you the exact moment when I fall in love with someone. It feels like an opening happening and the build of excitement and curiosity. It can happen across a crowded room or over and over with the same person you have spent your life with. It is something they do or say that causes this energy to burst forward, almost being the last drops of water to burst the floodgates open. I know many people who have said the same thing about the first moment. Shame we cannot feel so clearly when love is lost. In that situation, it is more like the flow of water turns into a trickle.

These cords become the conduit for that love, which explains why if we love someone and that person is away from us, we feel pulled around by them. That yearning can be a physical sensation in the solar plexus. There are one or two ways we can break these cords if the receiver of our love does not want us.

- Through meditation we can see these cords being cut by great giant scissors of light.
- Let time take its course.
- Not re-energizing them with love.

There is great romanticism in love that is lost; we don't always want to get over it. If that is what you are going to do be honest with yourself and then you won't give the friends around you such a hard time. Above all, jumping back into bed with this person is a big no-no, unless you do not want to lose the ties that bind you two together; after all, there is always hope. Even though a partner may have moved on and even found another mate, they might not always make it easy for you to break the cords. After all, the cords are a source of energy to them, and a link in telepathy between the two of you. Who does not want to feel the warmth of love? And when you remove the cords from a person, it does make them feel very cold.

Cord Cutting

The best way to cut those cords is through meditation and visualization.

Take a large piece of paper and write down the names of everyone you feel may still have an attachment to. Leave plenty of space between each name.

Take a pendulum, hold it over your hand and ask it which direction is yes, and then which direction is no. Then with that information, take the pendulum and dangle it over the names. Going from one name to the next ask the question, "Do I still have cords attached to this person?"

The pendulum will answer yes or no. If the answer is no then cross that name off your list. If the answer is yes, close your eyes and visualize this person before you, you can see the cords running between you. However you see them is right for you. Give this person a kind thought, then with a large pair of scissors made from light cut away at these cords until they are all broken.

If the cords don't break it may not be the right time for you to let go, and try this another time. When they do break, send a bit of healing love to yourself, and know that you have moved on. Intention is the key. New cords may form, but you always have the skills and tools to break them. You can do this with as many people as you like, including friends and family members.

How to cleanse your aura after accidental sex, rape, a break up or for a fresh start!

Most people have found themselves sleeping with someone and then regretting it after. Whether it's because you were drinking, lonely or it just seemed like a great idea at the time only to find out it wasn't. Wishing away that horrible dirty feeling that you feel physically and emotionally when you had sex with someone you regret.

This is also a good exercise for cleaning your spirit after rape or physical abuse. It's often said that you feel really dirty and no matter how much you wash you don't feel clean; this is because you still have the energy of what happened attached to you. It can be cleaned off even if the event was way in your past.

Just before you have a shower; ask for healing light to be sent to the shower, visualize the shower filling with light.

- Now when you take that shower see with the droplets of water, also the droplets of light coming down and cleaning your body and your aura. You can see this as a rainbow if you want to.
- If you don't have a shower, use salt crystals in the bath. If you can't get salt crystals from the shop you can use sea salt but not table salt. Salt absorbs the negative energy and then when you watch the water run out of the bath, you'll

know that all of the negativity is going down the plughole with it, and you are clean on the skin and aura.

The dark side of intuition

We can use intuition to know if the person we meet is right for us. We can use intuition to be able to tell if a person has positive or negative intention towards us, but in the same way a person can use intuition to tell if they can take advantage of someone. Intuition can tell you if someone is needy, vulnerable, gullible or soft.

Everything has a polar opposite. It seems that the light and dark, good and bad, right and wrong or even up and down, north and south, male and female have this polarity and difference in vibration so we can truly appreciate or understand the opposite. The dark side is described dark as it is dense in vibration. It is the opposite of love, which is a light vibration. Almost like the musical notes on a piano, to fully hear a high pitch you have to understand what it is not – a low pitch.

Any tool can be used in a positive or a negative way. Intuition can be used by others in a negative way to tune into how far they can push someone and manipulate them. You can tune into someone and use this ability to give them the love and build a great connection; however, a person may also use this to get someone to sleep with them who doesn't want to.

This is predominantly something that happens to women, but it also happens to men. However, men are less likely to talk about it. We all give out a vibration that people can tune into and know our emotional state or state of mind by reading us. Often these situations where we have been manipulated bring us out of the dark place we were in which allowed it to happen in the first place. However, it can compound the problem, making us feel that this is what we have to expect and suffer in our experience of sexual contact. This then means that we keep manifesting the same experiences proving our expectations are right.

There is a way to stop a cycle of abuse. The first is a little introspection about what vibe we are giving out that is attracting this kind of conduct. I am not saying 'blame yourself' but take responsibly for how you can change. A great example of this is when I was in my late teens and early 20's. I was new to London and had just come back from traveling. On my travels wearing a rucksack I had experienced having my breasts grabbed or touched. Backpacks pull your shoulders back and for well endowed women they are better than a wonder bra. However, this conduct was then happening even without the baggage and was continuing in my home country. I took a course with the Metropolitan Police in self-defense. I was unofficially taught how to split open a hand and break someone's wrist at the same time. This new skill has never been used. Knowing how to protect myself changed my vibration and therefore changed my experience.

If you are on the receiving end of manipulation or misconduct, strengthen your skills and the vibe you give out will change. This will then mean you no longer give off a 'victim' energy that could be used against you by the sexually unscrupulous. This is a wonderful tool to teach young girls, so they can feel confident in trusting themselves and their own intuition over men who would take advantage of their lack of experience.

Energy protection from ex-lovers and people with sexual desire

Most people have experienced thinking of someone, then the phone rings and it's them. So we understand that when you think of someone, that you send them energy. That makes sense when you love someone and you think of them, or feeling love when someone loves you. But what if someone is thinking of you when they are in a state of arousal? I believe this sends energy to you too. Most of the time it makes no difference and you wouldn't even notice. After all it would be very odd to have all these people lusting after you if you are an attractive film star; so most the time we are unaware. However, it may make you feel uncomfortable, especially if the energy is being sent with desire to control. It may make you feel better to have energy protection in place so we don't become the victim of undesired attention. There are many things you can do just by using your intention to move others' energy away from you. As you are fighting the energy of a thought, a visualization thought will be stronger.

- Visualize mirrors facing the person who you feel is sending you this unwanted energy, this will reflect back their thoughts.
- Visualize placing them in a giant jam jar, thus containing their energy away from you.
- By far the best thing to do is know that you are stronger and if you don't resonate with the desire, it just won't affect you.

I must stress don't get paranoid about it; the more you focus on it the bigger it gets. If you don't buy into it, let it go, they will soon find other people to focus on.

Author's Thoughts

I would love to not have had this final section in the book, and not to end the book on a low note. I don't want to give you anything but pure positive thoughts and love about relationships, so that in each and every page it brings a stronger manifestation of love in a written form. I would like the worlds of love to rub off on to your fingers and sink deep into your heart but you weren't born yesterday and you know things can go wrong. In this section I at least would like to leave you feeling empowered; that you are not powerless when things do go wrong. I hope you never have to find the parts written about in this section useful, but I would like to end it on a story of love of a lifetime, may you also live and love yours.

Jackie

I first saw him standing at the bar in a pub at a work's drink. Dark haired, beautiful smile …….. There was something about him; intuitively I knew there was something about this man, but I couldn't put my finger on it. A familiarity, a knowing. I watched him at work: he caught my eye, what a beautiful smile and kind face. He melted my heart. I listened quietly at work; he had been in a relationship and been very hurt. The tingles in the stomach, the butterflies; it was scary. Even now as I write about it, I can remember the butterflies. I had broken my ankle while out running and had been off sick from work. I remember seeing him drive past my house and waving and my heart missed a beat. It was electrifying. When I went back to work his best friend Martin told me that Andy "liked" me, my heart missed a beat, I more than liked him, and I suppose he was just testing the water. We were two souls attracted to each other. It seemed to take forever. I can remember standing in the yard at work during the early hours of the morning, looking up at the black sky and the stars thinking we were never going to see each other again, as Andy was transferring to a new job. The sadness in my stomach was heavy and lonely. I couldn't understand why with so much attraction this wasn't happening. I felt true sadness at the loss of something that hadn't materialized into a physical relationship. The bond spiritually was immense; the way I felt was overpowering. It was enough to fill the hearts of a thousand souls and yet we hadn't got it together.

Our first date, kind soft loving, it was very special. Like a 5-year-old with their first ice cream, not wanting to spoil it; oh it was pure bliss. Everyday was a spring day. I knew him, I loved him, I adored him and he loved me as equally, it was so overpowering. Sex was wonderful, the kisses, the touch, it was so special. I floated, just floated; we were married within 2 months.

Our first daughter was born 15 months later. What a beautiful baby, pure innocence. All she needed was love, warmth and care and there was an abundance of it.

What changed? My god, child birth! My body, my feelings about myself, I didn't look the same, I didn't feel the same. My little bundle of joy needed attention, my attention, oh I was tired. We did everything ourselves. We were renovating a house, working full-time, looking after a baby. Sex, what was that? My husband went off it for several months; seeing the baby born, he didn't view my body "as the same playground" that it had been before. Oh my god, I needed loving too! I was tired; it felt as if I gave out bags full of love. It's amazing how much love a human being can give. Sex was OK, but not the same. We didn't play, it was functional. It was something that just happened. How can you love so much, but not enjoy the physical contact... Baby number 2, a beautiful boy, 19 months between the two of them, how can you love so much? Well you can and more and more. It's wonderful, unconditional, two beautiful babies, pure innocence. Life and love, beautiful smiles that's what they both gave, I was truly blessed. How I loved those babies. Sex, what happened? Sex, what was it? Something of the past, the thought of it just exhausted my mind. That was the last thing I wanted. I didn't like my body, it wasn't the same. It didn't matter what I bought to feel good in, I just didn't feel good. I remember going to bed at night and my husband putting his arm around me and I would cringe. I knew he wanted sex and it was the last thing on my mind. The thought of it made me feel sick. I would deliberately go to bed clearly saying I was tired to avoid the physical contact. Why? Oh I don't know. The changes after childbirth are so immense. No time! Working full-time, studying for exams, looking after babies, housework, shopping, being a mum, a daughter, a daughter-in-law, a sister, the last thing on my mind was sex. My poor beautiful husband, oh he was doing his bit too, working, helping with the children but we just lost each other. We forgot about each other and soooooooooooooooooooo

Overcoming an Affair

One dreadful dark day, when I could bare the atmosphere no longer, us not talking, just caring for the children and working and building a home, I asked him what was wrong. He had been so horrible to me, I didn't understand. Nothing physical, he would never hit me, but not talking to each other, the atmosphere was revolting. There was no closeness between us, definitely no sex. I can remember cuddling him at night and him telling me he didn't deserve a cuddle he had hurt me dreadfully and he would never be able to forgive himself. I so didn't understand. And he told me, he had met someone else. My god, it felt like I had been stabbed in the heart. The pain, the shock, what? Met someone else? Who had he slept with? The questions going through my mind, the images, it was like watching a move, but it was a movie I was a part of. He told me he knew it was over. The pain, the pain, oh my heart broke. I left the house to go and see his best friend. He knew nothing about it and told me if he could do this to me I was better off without him.

I fainted. I physically collapsed. A strange thing really. I remember lying on the floor, seeing my body lying there and said to myself, get up, get up, and don't let him do this to you. But another voice was saying, but I don't want to get up, I don't want to. I don't know how I did get up, but I remember digging a hole in the ground and burying my wedding rings. It was like the end of something so special. I had trusted this man with my life and felt something had died that day.

The next six months, tears, pain, sadness, anger, hurt. What a roller coaster of emotions. The funny thing was, the soul actually craved it. The heart hurt so much. It had been broken, now I describe the pain similar to that of a heart attack. My heart always carries a scar, but it heals. God, it's amazing how love heals the heart. It heals the soul. It's deep, it's cool, it's soft, it's full of hope and trust, it's kind and warm, it fills you inside and out and it carries you through. My poor darling Andy, the pain he had inflicted upon me was overpowering. But the pain he inflicted on himself was worse. He had almost hit the self destruction button. It broke him. Six months of pain for both of us. When he called me and asked to see me, when he asked me to give us another go, I looked at him and felt nothing, and I couldn't tell him I loved him. I felt nothing and yet something inside me, this small voice in among the numbness of it all, said give it another go. He said he hadn't done anything to earn my love yet and I felt nothing. But I agreed to give it another go.

So how do you recover from something like this? You love, unconditionally, wholeheartedly. It's not about being a doormat; anyone who knows me knows I'm certainly not that. Friends, family they all have their own ideas and prejudices.

You're hurt, you are both hurt. Circumstances, stresses, forgetting each other, not loving yourself and then not being able to show love leads to a breakdown. It hurts, it hurts so much. But it heals. Love and time, and time and love, it heals. Working through it, forgiving unconditionally, loving unconditionally heals it. You don't forget, neither of you forget, but it happened to both of us. But in many ways it brought us closer. By not judging and condemning, leaving resentment and all those dis-ease feelings out of your heart can you truly forgive? And forgive ourselves we have.

Sex

Interesting, it was like starting over again. It took time and letting the world take a few turns, we overcame it. But when you truly open your heart I happens.

I'm really lucky. I love my husband; a little older, greyer, a bit heavier, he still has a beautiful smile and cheekiness about him.

Sex is amazing now. Why? I learned to love myself. We are all one, if you love yourself, you can love others. I need sex now. Good sex, fun sex, hard sex to ground me. To remind me I am human, to bring me back down to earth; and when you love a man, truly love him, even after all we have been through together, sex is fantastic. It's on a deeper, more spiritual level, it's two souls meeting and loving and talking and laughing and playing. Be true to yourself, love yourself, be kind to yourself, open your heart and allow the love to come in freely, it's beautiful.

Jackie, 43, Police Officer, London

Stay curious about yourselves, others and the world. When we stay curious with eyes open wide, we stay connected to love.
Becky Walsh

About the Author

Becky Walsh has her own practice as an intuitive therapist .
Author of 'Advanced Psychic Development'. Becky coaches
people in deep inner knowing and consciousness. Becky started
teaching at the College of Psychic Studies in London where she
taught intuition for many years. Best known for having her own
radio show on LBC 97.3FM. Gives talks and workshops around
the world and even performs her own unique show blending
Intuition, philosophy, spirituality stand-up comedy show. Becky
has features in many British magazines and is a media pundit for
intuition, spirituality and consciousness. Becky currently divides
her time between London and San Francisco.

Website: www.beckywalsh.com

For appearances and media enquiries please contact:

Martin Jeffrey

Email: martin@maje.co.uk or telephone +44 114 2764644

References

The Ultimate Guide to 21st- century dating by Carol Dix

The Power of Face Reading by Rose Rosetree

The Greatest Sex Tips in the World by Julie Peasgood

Simply Irresistible by Dr Raj Persaud

How to Have Great Sex for the Rest of Your Life by Val Sampson & Julia Cole

The Feel the Fear Guide to Lasting Love by Susan Jeffers

The Alchemy of Voice by Stewart Pearce.

The Female Brain by Louann Brizendine

The Way of the Superior Man by David Deida

The Sex Doctor by Tracey Cox

A New Earth by Eckhart Tolle

Take Me to the Truth: Undoing the Ego by Nouk Sanchez and Tomas Vieira

Other books by Becky Walsh:

Advanced Psychic Development O Books £9.99

Haunted West End Theatres (with Ian Shillito) £9.99

E-books:

Setting up a Private Practice: Beginners and Advanced.

Setting up a Private Practice: Healing Arts Edition, Beginners and advanced

Online courses:

Six part Audio Correspondence Course in Psychic Development

Six part Audio Correspondence Course in Mediumship

www.lightofspirit.co.uk for more details.

BOOKS

O is a symbol of the world, of oneness and unity. In different cultures it also means the "eye," symbolizing knowledge and insight. We aim to publish books that are accessible, constructive and that challenge accepted opinion, both that of academia and the "moral majority."

Our books are available in all good English language bookstores worldwide. If you don't see the book on the shelves ask the bookstore to order it for you, quoting the ISBN number and title. Alternatively you can order online (all major online retail sites carry our titles) or contact the distributor in the relevant country, listed on the copyright page.

See our website **www.o-books.net** for a full list of over 500 titles, growing by 100 a year.

And tune in to myspiritradio.com for our book review radio show, hosted by June-Elleni Laine, where you can listen to the authors discussing their books.